HOME WITH GOD

BOOKS BY NEALE DONALD WALSCH

What God Wants

Tomorrow's God

The New Revelations

Conversations with God, Book 1

Conversations with God, Book 2

Conversations with God, Book 3

Friendship with God

Communion with God

Conversations with God for Teens

Questions and Answers on Conversations with God

The Little Soul and the Earth (with Frank Riccio, illustrator)

The Little Soul and the Sun: A Children's Parable Adapted from
Conversations with God (with Frank Riccio, illustrator)

Meditations from Conversations with God

Conversations with God: Guidebook

Moments of Grace

Bringers of the Light

ReCreating Yourself

Neale Donald Walsch on Abundance and Right Livelihood

Neale Donald Walsch on Holistic Living

Neale Donald Walsch on Relationships

The Wedding Vows from Conversations with God

Honest to God: A Change of Heart That Can Change the World
(with Brad Blanton)

Meditations from Conversations with God, Book 2: A Personal Journal

HOME WITH GOD

IN A LIFE
THAT NEVER ENDS

———

A wondrous message of love
in a final Conversation with God

Neale Donald Walsch

ATRIA BOOKS
New York London Toronto Sydney

ATRIA BOOKS
1230 Avenue of the Americas
New York, NY 10020

The Library of Congress has cataloged the hardcover edition as follows:

 Walsch, Neale Donald.
  Home with God : in a life that never ends : a wondrous
 message of love in a final conversation with God / by Neale
 Donald Walsch.—1st Atria Books hardcover ed.
  p. cm.
  1. Death—Miscellanea. 2. Future life—Miscellanea.
 3. God—Miscellanea. 4. Spiritual life—Miscellanea.
 5. Private revelations. I. Title.

 BF1999.W2285 2005
 202'.3—dc22   2005054568

ISBN-13: 978-0-7432-6715-1
ISBN-10: 0-7432-6715-X
ISBN-13: 978-0-7432-6716-8 (Pbk)
ISBN-10: 0-7432-6716-8 (Pbk)

First Atria Books trade paperback edition March 2007

10 9 8 7 6 5 4 3 2 1

ATRIA BOOKS is a trademark of Simon & Schuster, Inc.

"Stopping by Woods on a Snowy Evening" from *The Poetry of Robert Frost*
edited by Edward Connery Lathem. Copyright 1923, 1969 by Henry
Holt and Company. Copyright 1951 by Robert Frost. Reprinted by
permission of Henry Holt and Company, LLC.

"The Impossible Dream" used by permission, © 1965, Joe Darion,
Words, Mitch Leigh, Music.

"Hope," from *Alive Together: New and Selected Poems by Lisel Mueller,* is
reprinted with permission of Louisiana State University Press.
Copyright © 1996 by Lisel Mueller.

Manufactured in the United States of America

For information regarding special discounts for bulk purchases,
please contact Simon & Schuster Special Sales at 1-800-456-6798
or business@simonandschuster.com.

INTRODUCTION

This is the word-for-word transcription of a holy conversation. It is a conversation with God about being Home with God. It is the last installment of an extraordinary dialogue covering nearly 3,000 pages in nine books written over eleven years and touching on all aspects of human life.

The present exchange explores many areas of human experience and, at a greater depth than ever before, one area in particular: death and dying, and the life hereafter.

The dialogue at one point journeys into territory lying at the furthest frontier of spirituality: the cosmology of all life. It offers a breathtaking glimpse of Ultimate Reality, presented through metaphor. It reveals in simple, accessible language the reason and purpose for living, ways in which humans may achieve the greatest joy, the nature of the journey upon which we are all embarked, and the extraordinary end to that journey—an end that turns out to be not an end at all, but an ecstatic interlude in a glorious and ongoing experience, the full description of which staggers the imagination.

The dialogue here is circular. It springs forward in spirals to astonishing new and never described or imagined places, then springs back to old ground to make sure the next mind-bending exploration begins on solid footing. If you will have patience with this book—and, by the way, with your life—it will reward you grandly.

The message of *Home with God* may be one of the most hopeful and helpful that humanity has ever received.

It is important for you to understand how you came to this conversation. If you think that you came to it by chance, you will have missed the enormity of what is happening to you right now.

Your soul has *brought* you to this conversation, as it has brought you to every other conversation with God you have ever had, in whatever form. It has contrived to place these pages before you. A myriad of circumstances were, just this moment, interconnected in a precise way at a precise time in order for you to be gently drawn to the words you find here, and only the intervention of your most holy soul could have produced such events so effortlessly. If you are clear about that, you will hear those words in a different way.

You have been brought here because the Universe understands that you have been quietly calling for answers to the questions all humans ask. What is really going on here in this life, and what will happen when this life is over? Will we be reunited with loved ones who've gone before? Will God be there to greet us? Will it be Judgment Day? Will we be facing the possibility of everlasting damnation? Will we be allowed to squeak into heaven? Will we even know what's going on after we die? Will anything BE going on?

Wrapped in the replies to these inquiries are enormous implications for every human being. Would we live our lives any differently if we actually had those answers? I think we would. Would we be less afraid to live as we were always intended to live—fearlessly and lovefully—if we were less afraid to die? I believe the answer is yes.

It hurts my heart to know that so many people feel frightened as they approach their time of passing into the next world, to say nothing of when they are in this one. Life was meant to be a constant joy, and death is a time of even greater joy, when it would be wonderful if all people could know only peace, and happy anticipation.

Like my mother. She was utterly at peace at her death. The young priest who went in to administer the Last Rites of the Church came out shaking his head. "She," he whispered, "was comforting *me*."

Mom had an unshakable faith that she was stepping into the arms of God. She knew what life was about and she knew what death was not about. Life was about giving all that you had to all that you loved, without hesitation, without question, without limitation. Death was not about anything closing down, but about everything opening up. I remember that she used to say, "When I die, don't be sad. Dance on my grave." Mom felt that God was by her side all during her life—and that this was exactly where God was going to be at her death.

But what of those who imagine that they are living and dying *without* God? That could be a very lonely life, and a very frightening death. In such a case, it might be better to die without knowing that one is dying at all.

That's how my father died. He got up from his easy chair one evening, took a single step, and slumped to the floor. The medics arrived within minutes, but it was all over, and I'm sure that my father had no thought that those were to be his last moments on earth.

Mom knew she was dying, and I think she allowed herself to know that because she could deal with it peacefully and joyfully. Dad could not, and so he chose to leave abruptly. There was no time to think, "Oh, my gosh, I'm dying. I'm really dying." Similarly, I don't think there were any moments during his eighty-three years when he said to himself, "Oh, my gosh, I'm really living." Mom knew she was "really living" every minute. She knew about the wonder and the magic of all of this. Dad did not.

My father was an interesting guy, and his thoughts about God, about life, and about death were a contradiction in terms. More than once he shared with me his total puzzlement about day-to-day occurrences, as well as his utter disbelief in anything at all happening after death.

I recall one striking exchange, two years before he died, in which he was reflecting on his existence. It was not a very long discussion. I had asked him what he thought was the meaning of life. He looked at me almost blankly and said, "I don't understand any of it." And when I asked him what he believed happens after someone dies, he replied, "Nothing."

I pressed for more than a one-word answer.

"Darkness. An end. That's all. You go to sleep and you don't wake up."

I was dismayed. An awkward silence followed, and then I rushed to fill the void with all sorts of assurances that surely he was mistaken, that there had to be an extraordinary experience

awaiting all of us on "the other side." I had begun describing to
him what I imagined that was all about when he cut me off with
an impatient wave of his hand.

"Horseshit," he muttered. And that was that.

I was astonished, because I knew Dad to be a man who, even
into his eighties, got down on his knees and said his prayers every
night. Who was he praying to, I wondered, if he did not believe in
a life that was holy and a death that was only the beginning? And
what was he praying *about?* Maybe he was praying that he, himself,
was wrong. Maybe he was hoping against hope.

This book is for all the people who think like my dad, for all
those who may be hoping against hope. It is also for those who
just *don't know* what happens after death, and who therefore have
very little foundation for understanding more deeply what happens in life, and why. It is for those who are not aware of any formula by which life itself works. It is for those who are puzzled, it
is for those who are not puzzled and think that they do know
some things about all of this, but who wonder once in a while if
they really are right . . . and it is for those who may simply be
scared.

This book is also for those who are not in any of the above
groups but who wish to help another who is, and may not know
how. What do you say to someone who is dying? How do you
comfort those who go on living? What can you tell *yourself* at these
moments? These are not easy questions. So you see, now, why
you brought yourself here.

It really IS a miracle that you found this text, you know. A
small miracle, perhaps, as miracles go, but a miracle nonetheless. I
believe that it is as I have said. I believe your soul drew you to this
book out of the same impulse that draws each of us onward,

to our next step, to our next understanding, and, ultimately, to the Divine.

None of us has to follow that impulse. We may change course at any moment. We may go in another direction. Or we may stand still and not go anywhere at all for a long time, stalled in our confusion. Eventually, however, we will all move forward again, and we cannot fail to ultimately reach our destination.

The destination is the same for all of us. We are all on a journey Home, and we shall not fail to arrive there. God will not allow it.

That is, in three sentences, the message of this entire text.

Everybody is doing everything for themselves. . . . When you understand that this is true even about dying, you will never fear dying again.

It is impossible to live or to die without God, but it is not impossible to think that you are.

If you think that you are living or dying without God, you will experience that you are.

You may have this experience as long as you wish.

You may end this experience whenever you choose.

I believe those are holy words. I believe they came directly from God.

Those words have been floating around in my mind for the past four years. I see now that they were my invitation. An invitation from God for a larger conversation.

You're right. I wanted to make sure that we had this larger conversation, and so I placed those words in your mind every time you thought seriously about life or death, even for a moment. This is a conversation you've been reluctant to have, and have put off repeatedly.

Yes, I know. It's not that I'm afraid to talk deeply about life, or even about death, it's just that these are very complex subjects and I wanted to make sure I was really prepared to enter into a huge conversation about them. I wanted to be psychologically and, well, I guess, spiritually ready.

Do you feel that you are now?

I hope so. I can't keep putting off this conversation forever. Even if I tried, you'd just keep placing those words into my head.

That's right, I would. Because those are the words I want you to hear even if you never get to the rest of the conversation.

Okay, I've heard them.

I want you to hear them over and over again.

It is impossible to live or to die without God, but it is not impossible to think that you are.

If you think that you are living or dying without God, you will experience that you are.

You may have this experience as long as you wish. You may end this experience whenever you choose.

Those words convey all that anyone who is afraid of living *or* dying will ever need to know.

Then we can end the conversation right here.

We can. How deep do you wish to go in your higher understandings? Should you choose to continue with this conversation, I will present you with 100 more words—a 100 Word Formula for All of Life.

Well, there's a tease.

> That's exactly what it was meant to be.

And it worked. I'm not about to cut the conversation short now. So here I am having a conversation with God about living and dying. Again.

> Yes, but looking at many things that we have never discussed before.

Who would believe this . . .

> It doesn't matter. You're not having the conversation for anyone else, you're having it for yourself.

I have to keep reminding myself of that.

> So often people see themselves as doing something for someone else when they're really doing it for themselves.
>
> Everybody is doing everything for themselves. When you awaken to this awareness, you will have reached Breakthrough. And when you understand that this is true even about dying, you will never fear dying again. And when you no longer fear dying, you will no longer fear living. You will live your life fully, right up until the very last moment.

Hold it. Wait a minute. You're saying that when I'm *dying,* I am doing it for myself?

> Of course. Who else would you be doing it for?

Once you answer most of the questions you've ever had about death, you'll have answered most of the questions you've ever had about life.

Well, we're off to an interesting start. That's a very intriguing statement.

> It is the first of many that will appear here. Yet our dialogue will go to places that will be not only intriguing but, for some people, unbelievable. Such will be the nature of the Remembrances for which you came.

The Remembrances?

> It is as I have told you in previous conversations. You have nothing to learn, you have only to remember. The conversation we are about to have, as with all of our conversations, will help you to do that. It will lead you through a series of Remembrances about life and death.
>
> You will notice that many of these Remembrances have to do with death. This is by design, for it is through

a deeper understanding of death that you will most quickly reach a deeper understanding of life.

Some of these Remembrances may be surprising, for they will challenge much of what you thought you knew. Others will not surprise you at all. As soon as you hear them, you will be aware that you knew that all along. Taken together, these Remembrances will bring you back to yourself, reminding you of all you need to know in order to experience that you are Home with God.

Humanity has waited so long to have a new conversation on these larger matters. Most of what we hold in our collective reality is from ages past. We could use some "new wisdom" here.

All human beings are born with all the wisdom of the universe imprinted on their souls. It is in the DNA of everything. Indeed, "DNA" could very well be used as an acronym for Divine Natural Awareness.

Every living thing has this natural awareness built in. It is part of the *system*. It is part of the process that you call Life. This is why, when people are confronted with great wisdom, it often sounds so familiar to them. They agree with it almost at once. There is no argument. There is only a remembering. It is part of their Divine Natural Awareness. It is said to be "in their DNA." It feels like, *"Ah, yes, of course."*

So let us now open this new conversation in earnest, allowing you to remember what you have always known. Let us talk with a fresh voice about these things, in order that you might refresh your cellular memory, that you might find your way Home.

I can be home with God while I am still alive, can't I? I mean, I don't have to wait until I die to get "home," do I?

> You do not.

Then—tell me again, so that I can clearly get it—why will so many of the "Remembrances" have to do with death?

> Death is the biggest mystery of life. Unlocking that mystery unlocks everything.
>
> Once you answer most of the questions you've ever had about death, you'll have answered most of the questions you've ever had about life as well.
>
> Then you'll know how to be Home with God *without* dying.

I've got it. Great.

> But I advise you not to have an expectation or to set up in your mind a requirement that everyone must "get" what is being said here, because if you do, you might wind up "editing" this conversation in order to be sure that as many people as possible understand it and agree with it.

Oh, I wouldn't do that.

> You could be tempted to, if you thought that others might marginalize it or ridicule it.

I don't think so.

> There will be portions of this conversation—especially when we get into discussing the whole cosmology of life—that will seem "way out" to many people.
>
> I have no doubt that the explorations and the mental excursions we're about to undertake will enhance your ability to deeply comprehend what is true about life and death—yet some of them may seem so far afield and so esoteric that you really could be tempted to edit them out.

No, that's not going to happen. My commitment to this conversation is to produce a faithful transcript of it, in its totality, leaving nothing out that you intend to be here.

> Good. Then let's get on with it.
>
> Here is . . .

THE FIRST REMEMBRANCE
Dying is something you do for you.

That's such an interesting thing to say, because I just don't see myself as "doing it" for *any*body. In fact, I don't see dying as something I am *doing* at all. I see it as something that is *happening* to me.

> It *is* happening to you. And, it is happening *through* you.
>
> *Everything* that is happening TO you is happening THROUGH you. And everything that is happening THROUGH you is happening FOR you.

I just never thought of dying as something that I was doing on purpose—much less something that I was doing for myself.

You *are* doing it for yourself, because dying is a wonderful thing. And you *are* doing it "on purpose," for reasons that will be made clear as we move deeper into this conversation.

Dying is a wonderful thing?

Yes. What you call "death" is wonderful. So do not grieve when a person dies, nor approach your own death with sadness or foreboding. Welcome death as you have welcomed life, for death IS life in another form.

Welcome the death of another with soft celebration and deep happiness, for theirs is a wondrous joy.

Here is the way to a peaceful experience of death— your own or that of another: know that the person dying is always at cause in the matter.

And that is . . .

THE SECOND REMEMBRANCE
You are the cause of your own death. This is always true, no matter where, or how, you die.

Do you think that dying is something that occurs against your will?

Gosh, you're certainly being true to your word here. That *is* going to be hard for many people to believe.

> There are some underlying principles of life—at which we will take a deeper look in just a bit—that may make it easier to hold some of these Remembrances more firmly in your reality.
>
> When we explore these basic principles more fully, you will come to know that what you call "death" is a powerful moment of creation.

See now? There's another fascinating thought. Death is a "moment of creation"?

> It is one of the most powerful moments you will ever encounter. It is a tool. Used as it was intended, death can create something quite extraordinary. This, too, will all be explained to you.

Death is a tool? Death is not simply a "doorway"?

> It *is* a doorway, but it is a magic doorway, because
> the energy with which you walk through that doorway
> *determines what's on the other side.*

Okay, okay, hold it. You're taking my breath away. Can we slow down here just a bit? Can we go over some of this one more time, and fill in a few of the blanks? What you just said there leaves me with a lot of questions.

> We'll look at all of them. We'll answer every one.

Great. So let's start with this idea of using death as a *tool.* That thought is brand-new to me. A tool is something that one uses on purpose. It's something that one wants to use. But I don't *want* to die. Nobody wants to die.

> Everybody wants to die.

Everybody wants to die?

> Of course, or nobody would. Do you think that
> dying is something that occurs against your will?

It sure seems that way to plenty of people.

> Nothing occurs against your will. That is impossible.
> So here is . . .

THE THIRD REMEMBRANCE
You cannot die against your will.

If I thought that were true, it would be so comforting; that would be so wonderfully healing to know. But how can I embrace that as my truth if it is my experience that *lots* of things happen that I do not want to have happen?

> Nothing happens that you do not want to have happen.

Nothing?

> Nothing.
> You can IMAGINE that things happen that you do not want to have happen, but this is not what is so, and it merely allows you to think of yourself as a victim.
> Nothing holds you back in your evolution more than this single thought. The idea of victimization is a certain sign of limited perception. True victimization cannot exist.

It's pretty darn hard to tell someone whose daughter has been raped, or whose entire village has been wiped out in a vicious act of "ethnic cleansing," that no one has been victimized.

> It would be nonbeneficial to speak in this way to people while they are in the midst of their suffering. During such moments, simply be with them with deep compassion, true caring, and healing love. Do not offer spiritual platitudes or intellectual excursions as a remedy for their pain. Heal the pain first, then heal the thought that created the pain.
> Of course it is true that, in the ordinary human sense, there are those who have been the "victim" of terrible occurrences and circumstances in life. Yet this experience of victimization can be real only within the

context of normal—and therefore extremely limited—
human awareness.

When I say that true victimization does not exist, I
am speaking from an entirely different level of awareness. Yet this is a level of awareness that human beings
can achieve, once their pain has been healed.

I think that your statements will be difficult for many people
to embrace, whether they are in emotional pain or not.

What I am saying here is nothing more than what
nearly all of the world's traditional religions have said
for many centuries. "Mysterious are the ways of the
Lord," they have proclaimed. "Have faith in God's perfect plan."

Later in this conversation we'll have an opportunity
to explore this idea of a perfect plan, and we'll also
take a look at how it is that many different souls inter-
act together to produce the individual and collective
outcomes of life on earth in a particular and perfect
way for a particular and perfect reason. In fact, I am
going to ask YOU to give ME an example of that.

You are?

Yes. And you will know exactly what I am talking
about when I do. For now, rest quietly in your heart
with the knowledge that all things are happening with
perfection.

I will try. I will try to hold that thought, and to embrace that
in my heart, as you have asked. But you're going pretty fast here.

You're moving pretty quickly. We've engaged in this dialogue just a short time, and already you're into . . . may I say it? . . . into the ozone. I mean no disrespect, but just where is this conversation going?

To where you have always wanted to go.

Which is . . . ?

To the truth.

There is no truth except the truth that exists within you.
Everything else is what someone is telling you.

Well, I've certainly heard that one before. Everyone and his brother is trying to tell me that he is leading me to the truth.

Yes, but only one person can take you there.

And who is that, you?

No.

Then who?

You.

Me?

Yes, you. You are the only one who can take you to the truth, because the truth exists in only one place.

Don't tell me . . . it's "within me."

That is correct. There is no truth except the truth
that exists within you. Everything else is what someone
is telling you.

Including what you just said right here!

Of course. Exactly.

Then what is the point of this whole conversation? For that
matter, what is the point of ever listening to anybody about anything?

I did not say that nothing exterior to you can *lead
you* to your truth. I said that you are the only one who
can take you there.

Yet if I knew my own way to the truth about life and death, I
wouldn't be asking you about it. I wouldn't be having this dialogue, now, would I?

A lot of people who I know would pray about it. They would
pray for an answer, for some guidance, in the face of their deepest
questions about life and death. And when people pray to God
for answers, and then they get them—often very clearly—they
say that God has answered their prayers.

You might say that this is the experience I am having here.
This feels to me, this whole conversation feels to me, like a form
of prayer, to which I am receiving an answer.

That's a wonderful statement, because it happens to
be true!

That's why I am keeping a record of this whole conversation,
of this whole process. I'm writing everything down.

Just be careful that this does not create in others the impression that clarity lies outside of them, and that they have to go somewhere else—to you, for instance—for answers. Be careful not to create a situation where others envy you for having found a way to wisdom, for they will then want you to show *them* the way, and that would be counterproductive, and could even be dangerous.

Dangerous?

The day that other people start believing that you have access to answers from God to which they do not, you'll become dangerous. So it's your job to do whatever you can to make sure that the world does not think this of you. You would be well advised to *not let the world make a special case out of you.*

Take whatever measures you think may be required to "de-specialize" yourself. You *are* special, of course. The idea here is to eliminate the thought in anyone else's mind that you are somehow *more* special than others.

What do you suggest?

Do something totally out of character for the kind of person that people may want to imagine you as being—something that a "saint" or a "guru" would never do. Manage a rock band. Become a stand-up comic. Open a bowling alley.

There are no saints who own bowling alleys? There are no gurus who are stand-up comics?

Are you kidding? They ALL are.

Ba-da-BOOM.

It's just that people don't *think* they are. That's the point. So, do something outrageous, something that will have people scratching their heads, something that will have them denying your specialness, and even accusing you of being very UNspecial.

Heck, just telling people the story of my life should be enough to get them to do that. I've made enough mistakes, done enough things that no one would approve of, to make it impossible for anyone to hold me in a very special place.

It is true that you are an Imperfect Messenger— which makes you perfect.

Because no one can confuse the Message with the messenger.

Not likely. Unless you allow them to. So just keep being human. Forgive yourself, and ask the forgiveness of others, for all your mistakes, old and new. Then go out and tell everybody that the answers they seek lie within them.

No matter which way you go, you cannot fail to get Home.

It's all very well and good to tell people that, but it's been said so often that now it seems like nothing more than a worn-out aphorism. I mean, "The answers lie within you" is just one step removed from "The force is with you."

Yet I am here to tell you that everything you will ever need to know, you knew at your birth. Indeed, you came here to *demonstrate that.*

These statements you are making are just so . . . I don't know . . . *disconnected* from our actual experience. How can I believe that every answer is "within me," and has been since birth, when I experience that I have so much to learn?

You have *nothing* to learn. You have only to remember. Life is a process of growth. Growth is the evidence of Divinity's presence and expression. *All of life works this way.*

Consider the tree outside your window. It knows nothing more now, when it is fifteen feet tall and covers you with the shade of its gigantic umbrella, than it did when it was a tiny seedling. All the information that it needed in order to become what it is today was contained in its seed. It had to learn nothing. It merely had to grow. In order to grow, it used the information locked inside its cellular memory.

You are not unlike the tree.

Have I not said, "Even before you ask, I will have answered?"

Yes, yes, but . . . well, I have to ask again . . . what, then, is the point of this conversation? Why talk to anyone about anything, much less pray or talk to God?

Even the tree needs the sun to spur its growth.

All of life is interconnected. No aspect or individuation of the Whole acts independently of any other aspect or individuation. Life continuously creates *interactively.* We are producing outcomes mutually. There is no other way We CAN produce them.

Your conversation with others, and all the information that comes to you from your outer world, is like rays from the sun. They cause the seeds within you to grow.

There are many things that exist in your outer world that can lead you in the direction of your inner truth. Yet even those people, places, objects, and events are only reminders. They are like signposts.

That is, in fact, what the "outside world" is all about.

The physical world is designed to provide you with a context within which you might Experience outwardly what you Know inwardly.

And so I actually benefit from the world around me showing up exactly as it does.

All humans do. That's why I have said, when you look at that world and all that has happened to you, "Judge not, and neither condemn."

Let us use the tree as our continuing friend in this portion of our discussion, helping us to find deeper understanding.

Let us imagine that you have walked out of the clearing and deep into a forest. You have never walked so deeply into the woods before, and you know that you are likely to have a little difficulty locating the clearing again. So, you place markings on the trees as you go.

Now, as you leave the forest, you see these markings and you remember that *you put them there* so that you could find your way out.

These markings are exterior to yourself. Ultimately they will lead you back Home, but they are not "Home" itself. The markings show you the trail, the path, the way—and the way looks familiar to you. You recognize it. That is, you "re-cognize" it, or "know it again." Yet the Way is not the Destination. Only you can take yourself to the Destination.

Others can lead you to a path, others can show you

their way, but only you can take yourself to the Destination. Only you can decide to be Home with God.

Your outer world is the path. It is meant to lead you
back Home. Indeed, *all the events* in your outer world
are meant to do exactly that. *That's why you put them
there.*

They are marks on the trees.

They are.

But if I put everything in my outer world into place so that I
could lead myself back to my inner truth—that's what you're saying here, yes—?

That's what I'm saying here. You have it exactly right.

—if I did that, then, in a sense, *I put this book into my own hands.*

That is correct.

I "caused" this material to come to me, exactly as it's coming to me right now.
It's a signpost. It's a mark on the tree.

Now you are seeing things clearly. That is precisely
what is so.

But then, if *everything* in my outer world is a signpost, how does
any single part of it have any significance? That would be like
walking down the street and arriving at an intersection, only to
see all the signs pointing in different directions, yet all of them
saying THIS WAY HOME.

Now you are *really* seeing things clearly.

What in heaven's name are you saying?

> I'm saying that no matter which way you go, *you cannot fail to get Home.*

Then it doesn't matter which path I take.

> No, it does not.

It doesn't matter which path I take?

> It totally, absolutely, and positively does not.

Then why would I bother taking one path over the other? If all paths lead Home, what's the difference which path I take?

> Some paths are less arduous.

Whatever you do, do not believe what is said here.

Ah! So some paths are *better* than others.

"Less arduous" is a factual description, "better" is a judgment. Which observation brings us to ...

THE FOURTH REMEMBRANCE
No path back Home is better than any other path.

Are you sure? Please, dear God, please, I need you to be certain about this. Nearly every religion on the face of the earth says exactly the opposite.

I say to you again, so that there can be no lack of clarity: no path back Home is better than any other path.

All paths take you there, because all it takes to get there is true desire, a pure and open heart, and faith that God has no reason to say, "No, you may not be with me," to any person for any reason, least of all because they've simply believed in God in a different way.

All true religions are wonderful and all true spiritual teachings are paths to God and no one religion and no one teaching is more "right" than another. There is more than one way to the mountaintop.

Religion was created by human cultures to assist those who are born into those cultures in knowing and understanding that there is an ever-present source of help in times of need, strength in times of challenge, clarity in times of confusion, and compassion in times of pain.

Religion is also a manifestation of humankind's instinctive awareness that rituals, traditions, ceremonies, and customs have enormous value as markers that assert a people's presence in the world, and as the adhesive that secures that presence by holding a people's culture together.

Each culture has its beautiful and singular tradition honoring a beautiful and central truth: that there is something larger and more important in life than one's own desires, or even one's own needs; that life itself is a much more profound and far more meaningful experience than many people at first imagine; and that it is in love and mutual concern and forgiveness and creativity and playfulness and the joining of hands in a united effort to achieve a common goal in which will be found the deepest satisfactions and the most wondrous joys of the human encounter.

Take then, each of you, your own path to Me.
Undertake your own journey home. Do not worry or
render judgments about how others are taking theirs.
You cannot fail to reach Me, and neither can they.
Indeed, you will all meet again when you are together
at Home, and you will wonder why you quibbled so.

Oh, and we have argued, haven't we? We have argued endlessly. We have quarreled and we have fought and we have killed
and we have died because we have insisted that ours is the right
way—in fact, that ours is the *only* way—to heaven.

Yes, you have.

Yet now here you come to tell us that "no path is better than
any other path." And I must gently ask, how can I believe this?
How can I know what to believe?

Whatever you do, do not believe what is said here.

I'm sorry?

Do not believe a single thing I say. *Listen* to what I
say, then believe what your heart tells you is true. For
it is in your heart where your wisdom lies, and in
your heart where your truth dwells, and in your own
heart where God resides in most intimate communion with you.

I ask only one thing.

What is that?

Please do not confuse what is in your heart with
what is in your mind. What is in your mind has been

put there by others. What is in your heart is what you
carry with you of me.

Yet you can close your heart to me, and many have.
And many also have closed their minds.

And please, do not tell others that unless THEY
believe what is in YOUR mind, I am going to condemn
them.

And finally, whatever you do, do not *condemn them
yourself, on my behalf.*

We keep *doing* that. We don't seem to know how to stop. And
we're putting ourselves through sheer hell.

Yet now here is the Good News: Humanity need
not go through hell in order to get to heaven.

We do not have to even walk *into* those confusing woods,
where we have to mark the trees to find our way out. We can
walk around them.

That is correct.

No matter how beautiful and tempting those woods may look
from the roadside, I don't have to step into the thicket, I don't
have to get lost in them and then try to find my way back out.

That is right, you do not.

Every day I promise myself that I am going to *stay on the path,*
yet every day I am tempted by life to get caught up in all manner
of "dramas" having nothing to do with who I am or where I am
going. Before I know it, I'm in the woods again.

And you're not out of the woods yet.

I know. I keep hearing the words of Robert Frost in my head. I've heard them before, but now I hear them in a new way . . .

> *The woods are lovely, dark and deep.*
> *But I have promises to keep,*
> *And miles to go before I sleep,*
> *And miles to go before I sleep.*

So come with me now. Let us journey together into the clearing, so that, at last, you can tell the trees from the forest.

Okay. On the journey to clarity we go. I have found myself in the woods, I have stumbled into the dark forest of my own conflicts and confusions, and I truly want now to get "back Home." But isn't the shortest path the better path? I mean, isn't shorter "better"? And what *is* the shortest path?

In order to answer this question we have to define what we mean by "Home." What, exactly, is this "home" to which people seek to return?

Most people think that "going home" means returning to God. But you cannot return to God, because you never left God—*and your soul knows this.*

YOU may not know this at a conscious level, but your souls know this.

But if my soul knows that I have no need to return to God because I never left God, then what is my soul trying to do? What is the purpose of life on earth, from the soul's point of view?

I can tell you in four words.

Your soul is seeking to *experience what it knows.*

Your soul knows that you never left God, and it is seeking to experience that.

Life is a process by which the soul turns Knowing into Experiencing, and when what you have known and experienced becomes a *felt reality,* that process is complete.

Home, it turns out, is a place called Completion.

It is the Complete Awareness of Who You Really Are through the Complete Knowing and the Complete Experiencing and the Complete Feeling of that. It is the End of the Separation between You and Divinity.

This Separation is an illusion, and your soul knows this. Completion can therefore be defined as the moment when Separation ends, the moment of your reunification with Divinity.

This is not really a reunification, because I have never *not* been unified, but it can *seem* like a reunification if I have forgotten this.

That's right. In the moment of reunification, what occurs is that you simply remember Who You Really Are, and experience that.

So, in a sense, *it is* a "returning to God," but in figurative terms only. In strictly literal terms it is a returning to your *awareness* of the fact that you never left; that you and God are One.

Yes! And returning to awareness is a twofold process. Awareness is achieved by Knowing and Experiencing, which produces Feeling.

Awareness is the Feeling of what you have Known and Experienced.

It is one thing to Know something, it is quite another thing to Experience it, and still another to Feel it.

Only Feeling produces full Awareness. Knowing, alone, can produce only partial awareness. Experience, alone, can produce only partial awareness.

You can Know that you are Divine, but when you Experience your Self *being Divine,* then your awareness is made Complete through the living of that Feeling.

You can Know that you are any *aspect* of Divinity— for instance, that you are compassionate—but when you Experience your Self *being compassionate,* then your awareness is made Complete through the living of that Feeling.

You can Know that you are generous, but when you Experience your Self *being generous,* then your awareness is made Complete through the living of that Feeling.

You can Know that you are loving, but when you Experience your Self *being loving,* then your awareness is made Complete through the living of that Feeling.

Many times I've said, "I just don't feel like myself today," and now I understand exactly what that's about.

When you do not "feel like yourself," it is not because you do not Know who you are, it is because you are not *Experiencing* it. You must add Experience to Knowing to produce Feeling.

Feeling is the language of the Soul. Awareness of Self is achieved through the *complete feeling* of your Self being Who You Really Are.

As Awareness is a twofold process, there are two paths by which it is reached. A soul arrives at Complete Knowing along the path of the *spiritual* world, and at Complete Experiencing along the path of the *physical* world. Both paths are needed, and that is why there are two worlds. Put them together, and you have the perfect environment within which to create Complete Feeling, which produces Complete Awareness.

Home, it turns out, is a place called Completion.

All souls find peace after their death.
Not all souls find peace before it.

That's a wonderful and comprehensive explanation of what is really going on in this experience we call life.

And we are nowhere near finished. The deepest mysteries of death are soon to be unveiled. This conversation has really only just begun to touch the surface.

Let us now examine your last question more deeply.

You have asked if the shortest path is not the best path back Home. The answer is, not necessarily. The path that brings you the most benefit is the path that brings you to Completion—however long that takes.

The moment of Absolute Awareness—that is, of Knowing and Experiencing and Feeling Completely Who You Really Are—is arrived at in steps, or stages. Each passage through a lifetime can be considered one of those steps.

No soul arrives at Absolute Awareness in one life-time. It is the cumulative effect of many passages through the Life Cycle that produces what might be called "Complete Completion," or Absolute Awareness.

Each passage is ended when the agenda or the mission *of that particular passage* has been completed.

This Life ends when you have completed what you came here to the physical world to experience *this time*.

You then add what you completed here to what you completed on other journeys through Time, until you ultimately "have it all together," and Absolute Awareness has been achieved.

So, there are two levels of Completion. Level One is when you complete a step in the overall process. Level Two is when you complete the overall process itself.

Yes. And the overall process is complete when Who You Are has been fully known, fully experienced, and fully felt.

This is a magnificent explanation, and I "get" it. There are specific things that souls come to earth to accomplish, to experience. Some souls may take longer to accomplish it. When they are complete, it is a time for us to rejoice, for their work here is done.

You *do* get it. That's great! That is exactly right!

And "shorter" is not necessarily "better." Being *complete* is the objective, not being *fast*.

Correct.

Terrific. Now I can feel good about myself again, because I don't think I've accomplished yet—and I am into my sixth decade—what I came here to accomplish.

And what is that?

I'm not sure.

That would make it very difficult to accomplish.

I know. That's part of my problem.

Perhaps we should talk about that.

I'm sure I would benefit from talking about that, but for now I really don't want to be distracted here. You were saying that, even though they may not necessarily be "better," some paths back Home are less arduous than others. I'm intrigued by that.

It is easier to take a path that has few obstacles.

Agreed. So how do I find one?

You don't find out. You create one.

How?

You're doing it now. By committing to even *taking* the path, you make things easier. Many people are walking through their life having no thought of being "on the path." They have not studied. They have not prayed. They have not meditated. They have not paid any attention at all to their inner life, nor seriously explored larger realities. You are doing that now. By

virtue of the fact that you are undertaking the explorations that you are undertaking right *here*—that you
are having this very conversation—you are creating a
path with fewer obstacles.

What I am saying here is that whether you take a
winding path or a straight one, go through the woods
or walk past them, when you get to your truth about
life and living and death and dying, you will have
cleared the obstacles and created a less arduous Path
to Completion.

Once you know about death, fully, you can live your
life fully. Then you can *experience* your Self fully—which
is exactly what you came here to do—and then you
can die gracefully and gratefully, knowing consciously
that you are Complete. That is a far less arduous path,
and creates a very peaceful death.

Something about this sounds like a judgment to me. Almost
like an imperative. "If you haven't died well, you haven't done it
right." That sort of thing.

You're making a judgment that I would never make.
There is no way to die "wrong," and there is no way to
not get to your destination—which is blissful reunion
with the Divine at the Core of Your Being. There is no
way not to be Home with God.

We are talking here about how to make your life
and your death less arduous, more peaceful. The statement to which you refer is an observation, not a judgment. If you easily move to Completion with what you

came to your body to experience, and thus die gracefully and gratefully, you have found peace before your
death, rather than after it.

All souls find peace after their death; not all souls
find peace before it.

When you die, it is impossible to not be Complete,
but it IS possible to not be consciously aware of this.
"Peace" is being consciously aware that you are Complete. That there is nothing more for you to do. That
you are done. Finished. And can go Home.

If you approach death in fear and trepidation, agitated and trembling, not wanting to let go, not feeling
finished, or feeling afraid of what is now going on in
your life, or of what is to come, you, too, will get to
your destination. *You cannot fail to arrive there.*

But it will be more "arduous," is that it?

That's it.

Let us make one thing clear here again. You are
always immersed in the Divine. You are immersed in it
right now. Indeed, you *are* it. You are Divinity, immersed
in Divinity, expressing Itself as the Individuated Aspect
of Divinity known as You.

Therefore, in the truest sense, you are not on a
journey Home. You are already there. You are Home
with God always.

You already are where you would seek to be. The
extraordinary secret is that knowing this immediately
brings you the experience of this.

Right now it feels as though we're going around in circles here. In this conversation, I mean. It feels as if I'm sleepwalking and don't know where I am.

> Not just in this conversation, but in your *life*.
>
> When you live—or when you die, for that matter—in fear and trepidation, agitated and trembling, not wanting to let go, afraid of what is now in your life, or what is to come, you are demonstrating that you do not know where you are. And the problem with this is that *what you demonstrate, you experience.*
>
> Ever it has been, ever it shall be.
>
> Therefore, you will not *experience* that you are united with the Divine, you will not *experience* that you are Home with God, *even though you are.*

Believe it or not, I am trying to understand. You're moving very fast, and this is very complex—as I knew it would be—but I am trying to understand.

> Good. Keep up with me, then. Keep tracking. You already know all of this. I am merely reminding you.
>
> You are not on a journey to the Divine, but you ARE in the midst of an eternal *process* in which you experience more and more of Divinity as you move through it. You are experiencing more and more of the Core of Your Being, more and more of the Essence of who you are, as life continues.
>
> You are eternally merging with that Essence—and, as part of the process of life, emerging from it again, as a replenished expression of it.

This process that we might call "energy merging" is the formula for all of life. It can be written as:

e+merging

That is why this event is sometimes called a spiritual "emergenc-y."
This is what death and dying is all about.
"Death is an emergency" because it is not about "dying" at all. It is about merging and emerging.

Do you mean that I not only go *into* total union with the Divine, but come out of it?

Yes.

Are we talking here about reincarnation?

In a manner of speaking.

Here we go again.

I think it is important to understand that none of this is reducible to one sentence or one word. Still, if you'll have some patience, I think you will find that none of it is beyond your comprehension.

All I want is to get to the truth about death and dying. I want to know "the God's truth."

You still think God is separate from you, don't you....

I don't really think that. I know that God and I—that you and I—are one.

Do you really?

I do. I know there's no separation between you and me. I know that I am an Individuation of Divinity.

Then why do you talk the way you talk? Why do you say that you want to know "God's truth"? You must know that God's truth lies within you.

"God's truth" was a figure of speech.

Ah! So what you are hoping to find, really, is *your* truth.

I am hoping to use this conversation, this "prayer," as a means of leading me back to the answer, the truth, which lies deep within me, yes.

Good. This experience can lead you to that path, but YOU must place yourself on it, as I have said now repeatedly. I can *show* you the way Home, but *you* must *take* the way Home.

I have said that in the truest sense you are not on a journey. You already are where you want to go. But since you do not know this, your *experience* is that you ARE on a journey. So, you must make the journey to find out that the journey is not necessary. You must embark on the path to find out that the path *begins and ends right where you are.*

You're afraid to die, and you're afraid to live.
What a way to exist!

How can I be sure that these words, out of all the words that have been spoken on this subject, can lead me to my truth about life and death?

> You don't have to agree with these words in order to be led to your truth.

I don't?

> No. Even if you *disagree completely* with the words here, you will be led to your truth—you will have found the path back Home, because if you disagree with the words here, you will then know *what you do agree with.* You will then take another path. And, if that other path is not your path, you will take another, and still another, until you find your way out of this confusion, and back Home.

I suppose that's how it could all work.

That's how it does all work. Your whole life leads you back Home, back to me. Therefore, bless every event, every person, every moment, for each is sacred.

Even if you disagree with that event, even if you dislike that person, even if you are not enjoying that moment, all are sacred, for Life informs life about life through the process of Life Itself, and there is nothing more sacred than Knowing, and then Experiencing, what Life has to tell us about our Selves.

And so, having this very conversation, even if you disagree with it, will lead you to your truth and your path Home. You will also be led to that path if you *agree* with this conversation. Either way, this conversation will get you where you seek to go.

All paths lead Home.

Every single one.

And each path has its own "marks on the trees" to help lead me there.

Precisely. Now you are understanding. Those are all your own markings that you see on the trees. Look around. Nothing is here that you have not placed here.

Yet sometimes you will not recognize your own marks. If you look at them from a different angle, they may look different to you. They may look as though someone else has placed them there.

We are talking, of course, about the marks of your life—particularly those that you would call scars. Be careful not to think that someone else has placed them there. That would turn you into a victim, and someone else into a villain. Yet in life, as I have already told you, there are no victims and no villains. Always remember that.

My wonderful friend Elisabeth Kübler-Ross used to say something about this that I really loved . . .

"Should you shield the canyon from the windstorms, you would never see the beauty of their carvings."

Yes. That is what I meant earlier when I said that all of life is wonderful, just as "death" is wonderful. It is all a matter of perspective. Perspective creates perception.

Yes.

No, no, don't just say "yes." Examine that last statement more thoroughly. Look into it more deeply. That is one of the most important statements I am going to make here. I said . . .

Perspective creates perception.

How we look at something creates how we see it.

Exactly. Thank you.

And so, if you look upon yourself as a victim, you will see yourself as one. If you look upon yourself as a villain, you will see yourself as one. If you look upon yourself as a co-creator in a collaborative process, that is how you will see yourself.

If you look upon every event of your life—including *death*—as a gift, you will see it as a treasure that will serve you always, and lead you to joy. If you look upon any event, including death, as a tragedy, you will mourn it forever, and receive nothing from it but everlasting sorrow.

Which brings us to . . .

THE FIFTH REMEMBRANCE
Death is never a tragedy. It is always a gift.

Focus on this now. Focus just on this event that you call "death." Because if you can see that this is true about death, you will soon be able to see that this is true about every other event in life.

And if I can see even death as a gift rather than a tragedy, then I can see everything else in my life—the "little deaths"—as a gift as well . . . all the so-called bad things that have been done to me, or that I have done to someone else. And then, there will be no more sorrow.

Not for you and not for anyone else.

When you live all your "deaths" well, you let others live WITH your deaths well. The little ones, and the big one.

Wow, what a thing to say. What a thing to slip in here. But it's not always possible to "die well." I'm talking about the "big death" now. I mean, sometimes we're just plain afraid to die.

Of course you are. And when you're also afraid of the "little deaths"—meaning any defeat or loss—you're also afraid to *live*. So you're afraid to die and you're afraid to live. What a way to exist!

So help us!

> What do you think I'm doing here? I'm spending time here helping you get rid of your fear of the "big death." Because when you are not afraid of *that*, you are no longer afraid of anything. And you can truly live.

So why *are* we all so "deathly afraid" of dying?

> Because of what you've been taught about death. Because of what you've been told.
> When you hold death in a new way, you can experience it in a new way. And that can be a great gift, not only to yourself, but to those you love.

I have a friend, Andrew Parker, who lives in Australia, and whose wonderful wife—"Pip" she was called by those who loved her—did just that. Pip died of cancer on New Year's Eve, just after the arrival of 2005, and Andrew shared with me an e-mail that he had sent off to a large number of his and his wife's friends. It illustrates perfectly what we're talking about here. In his e-mail Andrew said,

> Pip is the greatest gift I've ever had. She came to my life at a time when I thought I had it all handled, and didn't. She sat smiling in the moonlight that first night we really connected and I knew if I spent any time with her that I'd marry her and have children. What a blessing she has been! A cancer in her beautiful breast began the journey of our relationship, and oh, how her courage and strength showed me the way.
> Her ever-present smile and dry wit kept me on my toes, though it was her unconditional love that had the greatest

impact on me. Her love was as strong as a mighty oak, as deep and blue as an ocean and as powerful as the tides and currents within its depths. Unmoving was her commitment to me and how she saw me.

She looked past the rough diamond edges, the Newcastle drawl, the swearing and uncouth behaviors that were leftovers from my yesterdays. She saw only the best in me, and had a way of gently nurturing that.

Her treatments were brutal, as our primitive medical treatments are. Surgery, chemotherapy and radiation, hormones and early menopause never altered the feminine essence that was my love. The pain of such treatments never brought a moan of discontent, and with the birth of our children she glowed with motherhood, feminine energy and profound love.

All were touched by her beauty, both inner and outer. When we found out she had bone metastases seven months or so after the birth of our twins she apologized. It wasn't herself that she thought of in that moment, it was me and our three boys. And then she got up, dusted herself off, and turned on the love valve!

Having her second breast removed hurt her a little. It was her personal feelings about womanhood and having that taken away, though she was never more a woman to me than in those times post surgery. When we brought the boys in to see her the next day, she lifted, one by one, her children to her wounded breast, and never winced.

Her strength is burned in my consciousness, her selflessness and courage are my comforts in this space I now occupy, a space filled with her memories and still such a long way to go in my life.

In the next almost three years she lived. Oh, how she lived! With my business and career in tatters and my struggle to find myself, my path and direction, she quietly held space for me to grow. Nurturing my soul with love and acceptance and firm guidance, she never once let me get away with anything! God, how I respect her for that!

The last six months of her life seemed an eternity as I dwelt amongst the moments. Now I long for another moment in her presence. How I'd love her given the chance, how precious I'd hold each minute, each second, were I to have those times again.

Pip's last months and days were her greatest gift to me. Gradually, she stepped back from my life. No more fine dinners, it was my turn to cook and clean. "Who'll pick those clothes up if you leave them there?" ... her dulcet tones resound deep within my brain. I've the beds to make and the washing to do.

How joyously those tasks were completed by our Pip. She coached me with her beingness during those days, comforting me as I comforted her. I never felt closer to her and felt blessed to have the opportunity to serve her.

Then came the time to take her home, take her back to Perth and her friends and family. I glanced at her during our five-hour flight and the pain was evident. Such an arduous journey and none but me would know! She managed in her usual way, with the utmost dignity and care for others. Pip insisted we take her on the planned trip to Rottnest Island, swimming in the azure blue of the Indian Ocean still appreciating life's beauty and blessings, the simple things.

Her last days were a journey of biblical proportions, a

veritable forty days and nights in the desert. Her passing came when she selected her time, in her way. When she knew that it was to be all right, she gave me the greatest gift of all. To be with her, sharing space and holding hands when she passed away.

It was 12:50 a.m., New Year's Eve. She'd said she wanted to make it 'til the New Year rang in and she did, exactly. All of the pain of the vigil, all of the fear of getting it right, doing enough and saying the right things—all of it went with her spirit! Gently, just as she had been throughout her life, she left. And left me without a doubt absolutely clear about who I am and why I am here. Her greatest gift to me was *taking my fear with her.*

My days are now different, that's true, though she's never far away! Our boys are finding the going tough—a love such as Pip's is not easily replaced. We still grow together, her life's gifts like a Lotus flower opening slowly, petal by petal, as the forms of our lives take shape, fed by such a woman's love.

These words in my own way are meant to convey my tribute to my love, to the mother of my children, and to you, and to all. We are the better for her being here. I regret not one minute and I blame no one.

We are all at choice in the matter of our lives, how we act or react colors our existence. Pip and I chose our love, and tough as it was, it has given me my life. I choose to view it from the side of gratitude, not loss and pain. Oh, yes, they are present with me and are absolutely appropriate feelings. When you get past the fear you connect with love and with our own Divinity and oneness.

Love heals. It heals our souls, it heals our relationships, and it can even heal our planet. My wife gave me this love, and I choose to share it with you.

On New Year's Day I had dinner with the family, then I went to some of her friends' place for a few drinks. I left about 11:40 p.m. and as I walked the few miles back Home, Pip was with me. I felt the energy of creation and possibility, as people celebrated in their backyards, fireworks went off and Pip's angelic voice in my head said, ". . . and you were right, just as you knew you would be."

What she meant by that was that she was with God, in collective consciousness and once again at the seat of creation.

I cried.

There are no victims and there are no villains in the world.

This is a striking example, a wonderful, stunning example of how, when you live your death well, you let others live *with* your death well.

I hope when I die that I can do it as gracefully as Pip.

Having had the conversation we are now having will make a big difference. Knowing that you are dying because you choose to die will be a big help.

Everyone dies when they choose to die? Pip chose to die when she did? Terri Schiavo died the way she wanted to die?

Well, you know about Pip, because she actually *said* when she chose to die. She said she wanted to bring in the New Year.

Yes, but did she want to get cancer at that *stage* in her *life*? Did she really want to leave that early? Something like this would be really hard to accept by her husband, her children, and members of her family. They would ask, with deep sorrow, I am sure, *Why would Pip want to leave us like that?*

I have an answer that may shock you.

What is it?

Later. We need to talk about it later. There is much groundwork to be laid first. Then the answer won't shock you quite as much.

Well, whatever the answer is, I am sure that members of Terri Schiavo's family have the same question. They, too, I feel sure, would reject out of hand this notion of "pre-choice" in the matter of the timing and manner of one's death. No, no, most people would say, "That is not my experience. And that was not the experience of Pip or Terri, either."

I know you said earlier that souls leave their body only when their work is complete, and that this should therefore be a time of celebration, but a soul's leaving the body can still be very sad for the people left behind in the physical world—and telling those people that their beloved actually *chose* to leave could make it sound as if that person no longer wanted to be with them, and . . . well, that could be very hurtful, it seems to me.

I know a woman whose husband died when he was very young. The woman carried the sadness of her loss for many years. But the real loss was felt by her young daughter. She never got over the loss of her father—and, in fact, remains *angry with him to this very day* for leaving. She does not understand why her father would do that, and if I told her now that no soul leaves the body when it doesn't want to, and that every soul causes his or her own death and actually *wants* to die at that time, it would wound her even more.

> Unless she understood that he may not have *consciously* known what he wanted.
>
> That is not the surprising answer I am going to reveal to you later, but it is an important thing to consider as a possibility now.

I don't understand. What do you mean when you say that her father may not have consciously known what he wanted? I thought you've been telling me that everyone is the cause of his or her own death, and no one dies against their will.

> Perhaps it will help you to understand that human beings create, and also "know what they know," at three Levels of Experience—subconscious, conscious, and superconscious.
>
> Remember that I said, when you die, it is impossible to not be Complete, but it IS possible to not be *consciously aware of this.*
>
> A soul can know at the superconscious level that it is Complete for this lifetime, but not be "aware" of that at the subconscious or conscious level.

These three levels of experience were mentioned in an earlier dialogue that we had, which became the book *Friendship with God.* I found it utterly fascinating.

> At this juncture it is more than fascinating. It is important to understand, so that your questions can be answered.

Then let's go over it again. What are the three levels of experience?

> The subconscious is the place of experience at which you do not know about, or consciously create, your reality. You do so "subconsciously"—that is, with very little awareness that you are even doing this, much less why.
>
> This is not a "bad" level of experience, so do not judge it. It is a gift, because it allows you to *do things automatically.*

Like what? What do you mean, "do things automatically"?

> Functions such as growing your hair, blinking your eyes, or beating your heart are examples of things that you do automatically. You don't sit down and think, "I've got to blink my eyes. I've got to grow my finger-nails." These things occur—your entire bodily system operates itself—without specific conscious instruction from you.
>
> The subconscious also creates instant solutions to problems. It checks incoming data, then goes into its memory bank and comes up with rapid-fire responses to a myriad of situations, again automatically. If you touch a hot pan, you don't have to think about moving your hand away. You jerk it away in a split second. This is an *automated response based on prior data.*
>
> The subconscious can save your life. Yet if you are unaware of what parts of your life you have chosen to create automatically, you could imagine yourself to be

at the "effect" of life, rather than at cause in the matter. You could even create yourself as a victim. Therefore, it is important to be aware of what you have chosen to be UNaware of.

The Conscious Level is the place of experience at which you know about, and create, your reality with some awareness of what you are doing. How much of which you are aware depends upon your "level of consciousness." This is the physical level.

When you are committed to the spiritual path, you move through life ever seeking to "elevate your consciousness," or to enlarge the experience of your physical reality to include and encompass what you know, at another level, is true about you.

The Superconscious Level is the place of experience at which you know about, and create, your reality with full awareness of what you are doing. This is the soul level. Most of you are not aware at a conscious level of your superconscious intentions—unless you are.

The superconscious is the part of you that holds the larger agenda of the soul—which is to move to Completion in what you came to the body to experience and to feel. The superconscious is constantly leading you to your next most desired growth experience, drawing to you the exact, right, and perfect people, places, and events with which to have that, so that you may achieve the combination of Knowing and Experiencing that will produce Feeling—creating Awareness of your True Being.

The last time we talked about this I asked if there was a way to set the same intentions on the subconscious, conscious, and superconscious levels at the same time.

And there is. This three-in-one level of consciousness is called the *supra*conscious. Some of you also call it "Christ Consciousness," or "Elevated Consciousness."

You can all go to this place. Some people do it in meditation, others in deep prayer, others through ritual or dance or through sacred ceremony—and others through the process that you call "death." There are many ways to get there. When you are in this place, you are fully creative. All three levels of consciousness have become one. You are said to "have it all together." But it is really more than that, because in this, as in all things, the whole is greater than the sum of the parts.

Supraconsciousness is not simply a combining of the subconscious, the conscious, and the superconscious. It is what happens when all are combined *and then transcended.* You then move into pure *Beingness*. This *Beingness* is the Ultimate Source of Creation within you. You may experience this before your "death" or after it.

I assume this is how a living master creates.

Yes.

Then can a master ever be surprised?

For a person of continually elevated consciousness, outcomes and results are always consciously intended and never unanticipated. The degree to which an experience appears unanticipated is a direct indication of the level of consciousness at which that experience is being perceived. Remember that I said, perception creates experience.

The student of mastery is one who always agrees with the experience she is having, even if that experience does not "appear" favorable, because the student of mastery knows that she must have intended it at some level. That "knowing" is what makes it possible for one person to be utterly peaceful and "together" during circumstances that another would find very stressful.

What the student of mastery may not always see is the *level* of consciousness at which the experience was intended. Yet the student of mastery has no doubt that at *some level he is responsible for it.* It is precisely this knowledge that places him on the road to mastery.

Earlier you asked if Pip wanted to die, if she caused it, and I replied: "Not on a conscious level." Now you know what I meant by that statement.

All decisions affecting the human soul are made by that soul at one or more of the three levels of consciousness, or at the fourth level, the supraconscious level.

Pip chose the period of her life within which she was going to leave her body, as do all souls. In her case this decision was not made at the conscious level. Then, having made that larger decision *superconsciously,* Pip *consciously* chose the precise day and time of her departure—moments after midnight on January 1, just after bringing in the New Year. You can know that this decision was made at the conscious level because *she announced it in advance.* She was totally aware of what she was choosing and she created it.

Perhaps something like that was true about Terri Schiavo. Maybe she did not consciously choose the earlier events of her life, but maybe things changed when, after those initial events, Terri was said to have "lost consciousness." Maybe Terri had not "lost" consciousness at all. Maybe she *shifted* her consciousness. Maybe she "found" herself at a different *level* of consciousness—first, at the superconscious level, where she became fully aware of what she was creating and why, and then, finally, at the supra-conscious level, where, having completed what she came here to complete, she achieved Absolute Awareness of her intrinsic unity with the Divine.

I believe that Terri Schiavo used her life to invite the people of the world to move to a new level of inquiry about matters of life and death, the soul and God, and about what actions are of benefit to humanity in cases such as hers.

I believe that Terri Schiavo, at a spiritual level, was never, ever a *victim* of her circumstance. I believe that she knew during those final years exactly what was going on, and allowed herself to be subjected to it in order to draw global attention to herself for the good of all humankind.

I believe that Jesus did *exactly the same thing.*

Am I right about Terri?

It would be profoundly intrusive and inappropriate for me to reveal the inner superconscious or supra-conscious workings of this individual's mind. This much

can be said, however, and I have said it many, many
times before, about all human beings:

There are no victims, and there are no villains in the world.

Well, this is the third or fourth time you've made that statement
in this conversation alone, but I've said it before and I'll say it
again: the idea of no one being a victim is sometimes just emotionally difficult for people to accept.

You observed before that this is because most people are
looking at life's situations from the very limited perspective of
normal human understanding, but how can those of us who
seek to raise our own consciousness, and to assist in helping to
raise the consciousness of humanity, hope to enlarge that
understanding?

> Speak to humanity of the Tools of Creation:
> Thought, Word, and Deed. These are the devices with
> which you create your micro-reality. These tools are
> perfect. They are magnificently effective.
>
> What you think, what you say, and what you do cre-
> ates the experience that you call "you" and the condi-
> tions and circumstances of your life.
>
> It is as I said before: If you think that you are a vic-
> tim, say that you are a victim, and act as if you are a
> victim, *you will experience yourself as a victim* in spite of
> the fact that you are not.
>
> The same will be true when you decide to label the
> experience of others. If you think that another is a vic-
> tim, say that another is a victim, and act as if another is
> a victim, *you will experience that other person as a victim*
> in spite of the fact that he or she is not.

Do *you* experience Terri Schiavo as having been a "victim"? Perhaps you do. *Was* Terri a victim? No.

It is impossible to be a victim of circumstances you create.

Always remember that.

It is impossible to be a victim of circumstances you create.

Therefore, to be a victim of circumstances, you must swear that you did not create them. This tells a lie about you.

You create all of the circumstances of your life. If you create them at the conscious level, you will be aware of it. If you create them at the subconscious or superconscious level, you may not. *You will have created the circumstances nonetheless.*

All masters know this, which is why no master ever points a finger at another person and says, "You did this to me."

Yet you may experience whatever you choose. You may experience what you have come to know about who you are as a result of your life in the spiritual realm before your birth, or you may experience something other than that, something less than that. In this, as in all matters, you have free will.

This brings up yet another question for me. Is there consciousness before birth? From what you're saying here the answer seems to be yes. So we are "aware" of ourselves before we're "born"?

Oh, yes. Long before. The "you" that is "you" has been "aware" of Itself forever. We will talk more about this later, when we explore in more depth this matter of birth. For now, simply know that "YOU" have always been ... you are now ... and you will always be. When you are born, you simply disintegrate.

I what?

You disintegrate. You cease being integrated. You cease being Singular and divide yourself into three parts: body, mind, and spirit. Or what could also be called subconscious, conscious, and superconscious.

Oh, so *that's* the correlation.

Loosely, yes. Broadly, yes. It's not an exact, minutely precise correlation, but it paints the picture in broad strokes.

In this holy trinity—God in three parts—your mind is where your conscious activity takes place.

Therefore, think only what you choose to experience, say only what you choose to make real, and use your mind to consciously instruct your body to do only what you choose to demonstrate as your highest reality. This is how you create at the conscious level.

Look at this closely. Is this not what every master has done? Has any master done more? No. In a word, no.

*You are all At Cause in the matter of everything that is
going on in your life—including your death.*

10

That's wonderful. That's just wonderfully put. Thank you.
And now I'd like to return to something, if I may. Something a
bit disturbing.

    Please.

When you told me very early in this conversation that we are
all the cause of our own deaths, the first thing that came up for
me was that if this statement is true, then every death is, by definition, a suicide. I've been thinking about that ever since.

    That is not accurate.
    **The fact that everyone is at *cause* in the ending of
their life does not mean they are deliberately choosing
at a conscious level to do so. Nor does it imply that
they are doing so in order to escape some condition
or circumstance.**

Causing something and consciously *choosing* it can be two entirely different things.

What? I don't understand.

You can be the cause of an accident, but that does not mean that you consciously choose it.

Ah. I see what you mean.

So let's be clear about what is being communicated here. You are all At Cause in the matter of everything that is going on in your life—including your death. Most people are not consciously aware of this.

But if a person *is* consciously aware of this—and, by the way, this dialogue is *making* people consciously aware of it—then wouldn't *that* mean that when a person dies, that person is committing suicide? I mean, all people are, by these lights, at cause in the matter of the ending of their lives, no? Have I missed something?

Two conditions must exist in order to classify a death as a suicide.

1. You must be aware of what you are doing—that is, you must be making a conscious choice to die.
2. You must be making the choice to die for the purpose of escaping, rather than completing, your life.

One purpose of this conversation is to help you get in touch with the sacredness of your physical life; to assist you in coming to understand that life in the body is a gift of unspeakable proportions.

I said earlier that death is a powerful moment of creation, and it is. But it is designed for going TO something, not for escaping FROM something.

There's so much pain attached to suicide that I almost didn't want to bring this subject up. That pain is felt first, of course, by the person going through the turmoil that led to the decision to end his or her own life, and then by the family and friends of that person. Can there be any place of comfort in all of this—for anyone?

Comfort may come from knowing that the person who has committed suicide is all right. They are okay. They are loved and they are never forsaken by God. They will simply not have achieved what they set out to do. That is important for anyone who is contemplating suicide to understand.

Are you saying that those who commit suicide are not punished in any way?

There is no such thing as "punishment" in what you call the Afterlife. It is those who are left behind who are punished. They experience an incredible shock, from which some never fully recover. All of them feel an enormous loss. Many spend the rest of their lives blaming themselves. They wonder what they did wrong, they agonize over what they could have said that might have changed things.

The sad thing is that those who end their own life imagine that *they* are going to change things, and they are not.

Ending your life in order to escape something does not create a situation in which you escape anything. If you are thinking of ending your life in order to avoid something, you should know, I say again, that you are contemplating something that you cannot do.

A wish to avoid that which is painful is normal. It is all part of the human dance. However, in this particular moment of that dance a person is trying to push herself or himself away from something that the soul has come to the body to experience, not to escape.

Because that person has found the experience to be painful and difficult, he or she seeks to step into a void, where there is nothing to face and nothing to fear. But people cannot step into a void, because there is no void to step into. *A void does not exist.*

There is no void anywhere in the universe. Not anywhere at all. There is no "place where nothing is." Everywhere you go, the space is filled with something.

What is it? What is the space filled with?

Your own creations. You will face your creations wherever you go, and you cannot escape them—nor do you wish to, because you have created your creations in order to re-create yourself. It will not benefit you, therefore, to attempt to sidestep them, or to dance around them. Dancing your way to the void cannot be done.

Let me put this another way: A *Void Dance* is not possible.

That is very clever. That is a very clever play on words.

> I use words in this way frequently, so that you can easily and always remember the message they seek to convey.

Well, I will always remember that one. "A Void Dance is not possible."

> No, because what you die with, you will continue to live with.

That is a very powerful statement.

> It was meant to be.

Forgive me for going back to this, forgive me for saying this now, right here, as we are talking about ending one's own life, but earlier you said that death was *wonderful*. Why wouldn't someone whose life is terrible desire death if it is so wonderful?

> What you call "death" IS wonderful, but it is no *more* wonderful than LIFE. In fact, "death" IS life, simply continuing in a different way.
> I want you to be very clear here. You will encounter *yourself* on the other side of death, and all the stuff you carried with you will still be there. Then you will do the most ironic thing. *You will give yourself another physical life in which to deal with what you did not deal with in your most recent one.*

I will return to physical life? I can't "work things out" in the nonphysical, spiritual realm?

No, for it is the *purpose* of physical life to provide
you with a context within which you may experience
what you choose, in the spiritual realm, to experience.

And so by leaving physical life you will escape nothing,
but will just place yourself right back *into* physical life,
and into the situation you were seeking to escape . . .
except now you will be back at the beginning again.

You will not see this as a "punishment" or a
"requirement" or a "burden," because you will do this
all of your own free will, understanding it to be part of
the process of self-creation, *for which you exist.*

So we might as well deal with whatever we are dealing with
right now.

Indeed, *that is what life is for.*

When life is used in that way, you will die when you
are ready to use death as a tool with which to create a
new and different life. Suicide is the use of death to
escape, but it creates the *same* life all over again, with
the same challenges and experiences.

I've never heard it put quite that way. That says a lot.

Yes.

So, you may use death as a tool with which to
escape, or with which to *create.* The first is impossible,
the second is incredible.

But isn't there a bit of judgment in that? Doesn't that seem
to make suicide "wrong"? I mean, I thought that God had no
judgments.

There's nothing "wrong" or "bad" about creating the same life challenges and experiences over again. If you wish to face the same challenges over and over, go ahead and do it. In this, as in all things, you may do as you wish.

It is simply important to know, if you think that you are going to *escape* these challenges, that you are not. You are going to find yourself looking straight at them again. And, of course, that can get a bit repetitious.

What makes some people feel that they just don't want to face their present challenges anymore is the idea that they have to face them alone. This is a false thought, but it is held by many.

Loneliness is the biggest affliction in the world today. Emotional, physical, and spiritual loneliness—the feeling of being isolated and injured or burdened in a way that no one understands, and of being without resources—is a formula for hopelessness.

It is in the face of *endless* hopelessness that, at last, nothing seems to matter except escape. Yet you cannot and will not escape, but merely repeat from the beginning what you are seeking to avoid.

That is why I come here now to tell you that you are *not* without resources, *none* of you, and I ask you to announce this to all the world. You have but to call on me with absolute knowing that I will be there. You have but to reach out with absolute faith, to see me reach back.

May I ask you what may seem like a strident question?

Certainly.

Why do we have to reach out to *you* before you reach out to us? If you really are an all-knowing God, then you must know when we need help. If you really are an all-merciful God, then you must be willing to offer that help—*without our asking.* If we are already on our knees, bent over in utter defeat, why must we grovel even more and plead with you to rescue us? If you are an all-loving God, why don't you love us enough to help us without us having to beg you?

And while we're at it, what do you say to those who would tell you, "I *have* called out to you, and you have not been there! Do you think I have not asked for God's help? For God sake, why do you think I'm so desperate! I'm so desperate because it seems like even *God* has let me down! I'm utterly deserted here. And I want none of it anymore. I'm done. Finished. Through."

What do you say to *that* person, huh?

> I say ...
> I want you to consider now the possibility of a miracle. There is a reason why you have not experienced receiving a solution from me, but that reason is not important in this moment. What is important in this moment is for you to consider the possibility that now, right now in front of you, there is an answer. Open your eyes and you will see it. Open your mind and you will know it. Open your heart and you will feel that it is there.
> I say ...
> Only if you call out to me in absolute knowing will you be aware that your answer has been given you.

Because it is what *YOU* know, what *YOU* feel, and what *YOU* declare that will be true in your experience. If you call out to me in hopelessness, I will be there, but your despair may blind you, and block you from seeing me.

I say . . .

Nothing you have done is so horrible, nothing you have had happen to you is so beyond repair, that it cannot be healed. I can and shall make you whole again.

Yet you must stop judging yourself. The one making the strongest judgment is you. Others may judge you from the outside looking in, but they do not know you, they do not see you, and so their judgments are not valid. Do not *make* them valid by taking them on as your own. They have no meaning.

Do not wait for others to see you as you really are, for they see you through the eyes of their own pain. Know, instead, that *I see you now, in wonder and in truth,* and that what I see of you is Perfect. As I look upon you I have but one thought: "This is my beloved, in whom I am well pleased."

I say . . .

Forgiveness is not necessary in the Kingdom of God. God cannot be offended or damaged in any way. There is only one question of importance in the entire universe, and it has nothing to do with your guilt or innocence. It has to do with your identity. Do you know who you really are? When you do, all thoughts of loneliness disappear, all ideas of unworthiness evaporate, all contemplations of hopelessness transmute into wondrous awareness of the miracle that is your life. And of the miracle that is you.

And finally, my beloved, I say . . .

You are surrounded in this very moment by a hundred thousand angels. Accept, now, their ministrations. And then, pass their gifts on to others. For it is in giving that you shall receive, and it is in healing that you shall be healed. The miracle for which you have been waiting has been waiting for you. You will know this when you become the miracle that *another* awaits.

Go then and perform your miracles, and allow your death to be the moment of your greatest glory, not an announcement of your greatest sorrow. Use death as a tool with which to create, not with which to destroy, with which to move forward, not with which to go back. In this choice will you have honored Life Itself, and allowed Life to bring you your own grandest dream, even while you are living with your physical body: peace within your soul at last.

Thank you.

Thank you for those words.

I hope and pray they may be heard by every hurting person.

I need to ask you one more question about all this. What about when a person asks another—a doctor or a loved one—to assist them in bringing their life to an end?

You are speaking of euthanasia, which is quite a different thing. This is when a person realizes that her or his life is already over in every practical way, and that there is nothing left to experience except unremitting physical pain or total loss of dignity in the death process.

Euthanasia cannot be equated with suicide. People who are contemplating suicide in the middle of an otherwise active and reasonably healthy life are making a very particular kind of decision. People who end a life that is a very short time away from ending anyway, with every medical evidence indicating that, are making an entirely different kind of decision.

Those who see clearly by every medical evidence that their physical life is all but over may choose to ask, "Is it necessary to suffer this final pain and indignity?" Each soul will have an answer that is right for it, and no soul will answer the question incorrectly—because there is no such thing as an "incorrect" answer.

I see the difference clearly, and I think every reasonable person does.

You are different from God, but you are not divided from God. That is why you can never die.

II

Now let me return, please, to something else. You said earlier that you would describe some basic spiritual principles of life that would make it easier for us to understand life itself, and death. And while you've since touched on several, is there any one single basic life principle that could just throw open wide the door to deeper understanding in one moment?

Yes. And this is ...

THE SIXTH REMEMBRANCE
You and God are one. There is no separation between you.

While this may appear to some to be a very elementary piece of information, when you apply this basic principle of life TO life, you create a container within which you can hold all the previous Remembrances you've brought yourself here, as well as those to come.

The implications of the Sixth Remembrance are enormous. If you are clear that you and God are one, and that there is no separation between you, it changes the context within which you experience that everything in your life has happened, is happening, and ever will happen.

To use obvious examples from what we have just been talking about here, an understanding of your unity with the Divine makes it far less arduous for you to remember and embrace the truth that you are the cause of your own death, or that there are no victims and no villains in the world. This can make your path to Completion less arduous, and your death more peaceful.

Now obviously, the individual that is "you" does not represent the Totality of God. Yet you have all the characteristics, all of the aspects, all of the elements of Divinity within you.

God is you, writ large. Indeed, God is everything. There is nothing that is *not* God.

I've often heard the analogy that I am, to God, as a wave is to the ocean. The same stuff, exactly. Just smaller in size.

That analogy has indeed been used many times, and it is not inappropriate.

So now, let us define this "ocean." Let us propose here that God is the Creator. Very few people who believe in a God at all have an argument with that.

> If it is true that God is the Creator, this means that you, too, are a creator. God creates *all* of life, and you create all of *your* life. It's that simple.
>
> If you think of it that way, you can hold it in your consciousness.
>
> You and God are creating all the time—you on the micro level, God on the macro. Are you clear?

Yes, I see! There is no separation between the wave and the ocean. None. The wave is one *part* of the ocean, *acting in a certain way.* The wave does the same thing the ocean does, in smaller degree.

> That is exactly correct. You are me, acting the way you are acting. I give you the power to act as you are acting. Your power comes from me.
>
> Without the ocean, the wave does not have the power to be a wave. Without me, you do not have the power to be you. And without you, my power is not made manifest.
>
> Your joy is to make me manifest. *The joy of humanity is to manifest God.*

Now there's a statement.

> Here's another ...
> *Life is God, made physical.*
> What is important to understand is that there is no single way in which life makes God physical. Some waves are small, barely a ripple, while other waves are huge, thunderous in their sweep. Yet, whether minuscule or monstrous, there is always a wave. There is no

time when there is not a wave on the ocean. And while every wave is different, not a single one is divided from the ocean itself.

Difference does not mean *division*. Those words are not interchangeable.

You are different from God, but you are not divided from God. The fact that you are not divided from God *is why you can never die.*

The wave lands on the beach, but it does not cease to be. It merely changes form, receding back into the ocean.

The ocean does not get "smaller" every time a wave hits the sand. Indeed, the incoming wave demonstrates, and therefore reveals, the ocean's majesty. Then, by receding into the ocean, it restores the ocean's glory.

The presence of the wave is evidence of the existence of the ocean.

Your presence is evidence of the existence of God.

I should tack that to my refrigerator. YOUR PRESENCE IS EVIDENCE OF THE EXISTENCE OF GOD. What a great bumper sticker! This explanation is so simple, and yet so elegant.

So when we say that "God, and God alone" chooses the time of our death, we are saying that humans are part of that process, because humans are part of God.

Yes, that is exactly right.

And when I die, my death will be happening *through me,* not *to me.*

That is correct. You are now looking at it in a different way. You are changing your perspective. This will

change your perception. And it will alter your experience. Perception creates experience.

But there is just one last thing that I can't yet put together. Why in the world would I choose to die, ever?

Oh, that's simple.
Because you're done. Finished. Complete.

There are those who say that seeing is believing.
I am telling you that believing is seeing.

Well, okay, we've kind of circled back again. Am I understanding you to say that I came here with something I have to do? And that when I do what I came to do, I am finished, and ready to leave?

> It's not something you have to do, it is something you choose to experience.
>
> If you and God are One, you don't *have to do* anything. Every decision emerges from Free Will. Every choice demonstrates it.
>
> You have come to the body to experience an aspect of yourself, as we discussed earlier. It could be that this aspect of you is experienced through something you do—that is, through a physical activity—or through some particular way that you are being, even if you are actually doing nothing.

I need an example of that to make it more real.

Well, since we are talking a lot about what you call "death" and "dying" here, let's say that you are sitting quietly at a funeral. You are doing nothing, really, except sitting there. You are hardly moving. But you are being something, yes?

Maybe you are being sad. Or maybe you are being inwardly joyous. You could be either. Much would depend on how you see things—in this case, on how you see "death."

My perspective will create my perception.

Yes, and this is the way you create what you are being. In short, if you are being sad, it is because of the way you are looking at things. And if you are being inwardly joyous at that funeral, it is for exactly the same reason. And how you are looking at things is a choice *you make*. It is a Free Will Choice that defines who you are and who you wish to be, and how you wish to experience yourself.

You can change your perspective in any situation by changing your mind about how you want to "look at it." You can decide what you want to see, and then, having placed it there, you will find it there.

Now *there's* a statement.

Yes. It is a very empowering statement of what is so—unless it is not. And do you know who will decide?

Me.

Yes, you. That is right. You will decide. You will decide whether that is a very empowering statement *by how you see it*. And so, the effect is circular. What you see is what you get, and what you get is what you see.

You see?

Cute. Very cute.

Believe it or not, there is more going on here than my simply being glib.

Oh, I know that. Your glibberosities always point to a huge underlying truth.

I'm glad you like making up words. That's going to come in handy later.

So, getting back to our example, one way for me to be inwardly joyous as I near the time of my *own* funeral is for me to understand that when I die, it is because I choose to die. Everything that happens to me, I am, at some level, causing—including my own death, and the timing of it.

That is exactly what I am saying here, yes. This will bring you great peace at the time of your death. Knowing that you and God are One, and that you are making this decision jointly, can take you to a place of soft serenity.

Yet that idea requires humanity to believe in a whole different kind of universe. In our universe, most people who believe in God at all think of God, not themselves, as First Cause. And God is certainly the cause of their death. They die when God decides to "call them Home."

They die when THEY decide to GO Home.

You are asking me to believe in a universe in which I am the cause of my own experience, absolutely.

That is the universe in which you live.

It doesn't appear that way.

And it will not appear that way until you change your perspective. Nothing will appear that you cannot see.

Well, there's wisdom for you.

More wisdom than you know. There are those who say that seeing is believing. I am telling you that *believing is seeing*.

I love that new twist on that old aphorism. And this, too, you have said before.

And I will say it again, until you get it.

Okay, so no one dies "before his time." You've said it over and over here, so I guess I have to either accept this or reject the entire notion. I'm going to accept it as true, even though it is difficult for me to do so.

Tell me why that is so difficult.

I guess I've still been clinging to the notion . . . look, I've heard all that you've just said, but . . . I guess there is a part of me that's still clinging to the notion that things happen to us that we do not want to have happen, that "stuff happens" that we do not create within ourselves. But I get now that nothing happens by chance, and so, no one dies when he or she does not choose to die.

> **There is no such thing as "not choosing." *Everything* is chosen.**

Yes, okay, I see. And I guess you do have to keep making this point over and over again, because it runs counter to everything humanity has ever told itself about all this. And I have to tell you something. Just as I am writing this, just as we are engaging in this very specific part of what I expect to be a very long conversation, Life Itself is contriving to make me more and more clear that what you are saying is true. Nothing happens by chance. I mean, my life itself, *my everyday life,* is convincing me of this—and it is doing so at this very moment.

> **Tell me about that.**

Can it possibly be "by chance" that, just as we were having the exact exchange above, I took a short break from my writing and, for a change of pace, decided to open my mailbox, only to find a letter from a reader?

The letter writer, Jackie Peterson (whose name I've changed to protect this person's identity), wrote to me saying that she had just lost her fiancé two months ago from a massive heart attack. She was devastated, especially since her fiancé had always been healthy; he always passed his checkups with a clean bill of health.

She mentioned the *Conversations with God* books, in which she read that we choose our earthly life situations. So she wonders: has she chosen this situation for herself—or is it part of her former fiancé's model of life?

Did you reply to that letter?

I sure did. After I got over being completely flabbergasted that it would just "show up" at this exact moment, I did my best to answer the question. I based my reply on the very conversation we are having right now.

Well, let's see how you did. Let's see what you wrote.

This is my reply . . .

My Dear Jackie,

Please hear me at the depth of your soul when I tell you how sorry I am that this has occurred in your life. I do not want to give you "easy answers" here that make it all sound so simple and make you wonder why any of this should be a problem . . .

Jackie, this IS a problem, and a huge sadness, and you have every right to feel the way you are feeling, which is angry and sad and confused and frustrated and searching for answers.

The first thing that I want to advise is that you allow yourself to have all the feelings that you are having, without trying at any level to control or regulate or limit or restrict them. Just *have your feelings* and let them be what they are from moment to moment.

It is remarkable that you should present me with this question today, because I am just now bringing through my next *CwG* dialogue book, called *Home with God in a Life That Never Ends*. And in that book I was *just now* exploring this idea of the soul choosing when it is going to leave the body and return Home.

And yes, it is true that in this latest *CwG* book, as in all the others, God is telling us that nobody dies at a time or in a way that is not of his or her own choosing. Yet God also makes it clear that this may not be a *conscious* choice, but may have been chosen at a level of awareness to which only the Soul has access.

If this is the case, it would mean that your fiancé did not choose at a conscious level to die when he did. At that level, his death may have been as much a surprise to him as it was to you. I suspect that it was. I do not believe that your fiancé *consciously chose* to leave you.

It is true in my awareness that sometimes the Soul chooses things at a subconscious or a superconscious level that it would never choose at a conscious level, and that it does this in order to fulfill its Larger Agenda. Dying nearly always falls into this category. Very few people choose to die when and where and how they do, consciously. I believe that Christ did. I believe that the Buddha did. I believe that other souls have done so, but I believe that this circumstance is very rare.

Try, therefore, not to be too angry with your fiancé, but rather, allow yourself to direct your anger toward the *circumstance* that took him away from you just as you were really beginning to enjoy your life together. I deeply understand and appreciate how devastated you are, and as I said, you have a right to be.

In terms of understanding all that has happened, however, I believe that it is possible that one of the goals of the soul of your fiancé was to experience itself in Perfect Union and Wonderful Relationship, after many attempts in this lifetime, and many attempts in previous lifetimes as well. I believe that your fiancé was a gift to you—and that you were an even more extraordinary gift to him. You were what he, too, had been searching for.

I believe you entered his life as part of a "contract" or "agreement," allowing him to experience himself, at last, as much, much more of Who He Really Is. I believe that he felt more "himself" with you than with anyone else he was ever with. Not only in this lifetime, but, perhaps, in many, *many* lifetimes.

This may all be a little hard to take, Jackie, on a human level—so I am going to ask you to see if you can "jump" to a very high spiritual level to understand what I am going to say next: I believe it is possible that your fiancé died of happiness.

You are right, Jackie, he never did have a seriously ill day in his life. He was in good condition, he did have his checkups regularly, etc., and there was no earthly reason for him to die so suddenly. There may, however, have been a spiritual reason.

He may, quite simply, have finally finished his earthly agenda—with your help; with the assistance of you, the Friendly Soul with the *specific intention* of providing him that last assistance so that he could return Home, and then move forward with his evolution.

You showed this wonderful man, Jackie, just how wonderful relationship could be, and just how wonderful HE could be inside a relationship. As I said, Jackie, I believe that your relationship created a context within which he could have an experience of himself unlike any he had ever had before. I will go further. I am willing to bet that he actually *told you this*. I am sitting here believing that he actually said this to you in so many words—that he never experienced himself before the way he experienced himself with you.

And so, Jackie, your fiancé left his body suddenly, gloriously celebrating what he had found and what he had finally experienced of himself: the fullness of Who He Is.

The great sadness that you are being asked to bear is all part of the enormous, unspeakably wonderful and spiritually generous gift that you have been invited by Life to give this very special "other" (which is really just another part of you) so that you, *also,* may know Who You Really Are.

For your fiancé gave *you* a treasure as well (*CwG* says: "All true benefits are mutual"), which is the knowledge that you are capable of giving, receiving, and experiencing a wondrous love in human form—something that you had seriously begun to doubt before he came along. His intention, then, was to *give you back to yourself.* And this he did.

And so, the Divine Purpose for your relationship has been served and was completed in Divine Form and with Divine Timing. The beginning of your relationship in this form was by Divine Timing (as I am sure you know, because I believe you both talked about this often), and the ending of your relationship in this form was equally by Divine Timing, although I know it is very difficult to see or experience this right now.

I believe that you may be preparing to serve an even larger agenda in the years ahead, using this experience to bring help and healing to others who find themselves in many different life situations, each of which will be challenging to them at a spiritual level. I believe that you may be preparing to move forward in the joy of giving people back to themselves.

Some of these others whom you will encounter may be

people who have lost their belief in love, who think that the right and perfect relationship is simply not possible or open to them, and who think they would be better to just forget the whole idea as a great hoax of the universe. You will be able to tell them differently, and encourage them to remain open, always, to the possibility.

Some of these others may be people who find themselves in sudden bereavement, who do not understand and cannot "see the perfection" in the moment at hand, but only experience the loss and the pain, and who may even believe that they simply cannot go on. You will be able to tell them differently, and encourage them to remain open, always, to the next grand gift of life, and to the next extraordinary moment of knowing and to expressing their highest notion of themselves, of God, of love, and of Who They Really Are.

Of course, all of this is conjecture on my part. I could be "making it all up," Jackie, and I admit that. But I always see a larger purpose and a larger agenda at play in life's events—including life's most tragic events, and life's saddest. I believe that at the end of our lives in our present physical form, all of this will become instantly and joyously clear to us, and we will rejoice and be glad in the perfect symmetry of it all.

I also believe, Jackie, that your relationship with your fiancé can never end, and that he is able to be there with you at any time you wish to call on his love and his spiritual energy to help you as you continue your journey, even as he continues his.

I believe that your journeys will always be together, even as they have been together for eons past. This is not the first time the two of you have been together in physical form—and this, too, is something that I believe you both recognized and understood. Nor, my dear Jackie, will it be the last. Indeed, your relationship never ends, *ever*.

It is ongoing even now, even in this very moment—for who do you think it is that brings you these words? Do you imagine it is me? Or could it be some other, speaking *through* me, bringing this message to you?

Do you believe that such a thing is possible, Jackie? Because, you see, I do.

Do not seek to "not be sad," Jackie, during this time of loss. Sadness is one of the heart's ways of honoring another. So, too, is happiness. You honor the soul of your beloved, Jackie, by feeling your sadness fully now. And you will honor the soul of your beloved, Jackie, by feeling your happiness fully, too, when the day and time for that comes—as surely it will.

As we await that day, my wish for you is to find peace for your soul, Jackie. May the peace that passeth all understanding be with you, and abide with you, both now, and even forevermore.

I flow my love to you on wings of prayer.

Neale

Objective observation is impossible. Nothing which is observed is unaffected by the observer.

13

I see that you have deeply internalized what you have remembered.

You understand clearly now.

Thanks to you, I think I do. I think I've finally grasped, and really *understood,* the truth.

Be careful. You mean *your* truth, right? THE truth does not exist as an objective reality.

Perspective creates perception, and perception creates experience. The experience that perception creates for you is what you call "truth."

Your truth is what you actually experience. Everything else is what someone else has experienced—*and has told you about.*

This has nothing to do with you.

There is no such thing as objective reality?

No. "Objective reality" is an oxymoron.

Are you saying that nothing is as it appears?

> I am saying just the opposite. *Everything* is as it appears. And appearances are based on perceptions. And perceptions are based on perspectives, and perspectives are not objective. They are subjective. They are not something that you experience, they are something that you *choose.*

You just said this a moment ago. It was hard for me then, and it's hard for me now. I choose to have the perspectives that I have?

> You do, indeed.
> *That is the process by which you create.*

That's very difficult for me to believe.

> Then you will not believe it.

With the result that—

> —you will not experience it.

So if I don't *believe* that I choose to have any perspective that I wish, then I cannot *have* any perspective that I wish.

> Just so.

Because that is my perspective.

> Because that is your perspective.
> And that will change your perception, which will change your experience—and your experience will reinforce your perspective.

But I could argue that I did not *choose* that perception. It is simply what I observe, objectively.

> It is what you observe, *given your perspective*.
> You observe nothing "objectively."
> Objective observation is impossible.

Another oxymoron. "Objective observation" is an oxymoron.

> Yes.
> *Nothing that is observed is unaffected by the observer.*

I'm sure that sounds like a lot of new age spiritual gobbledygook to many people.

> That's interesting, because it's pure science.

Science?

> It is elementary quantum physics. Read any book on quantum mechanics.

So you're saying that I affect what I see by the very way that I look at it?

> *Or whether you look at it at all.* That's exactly what I'm saying. That is precisely the case.

Well, we've certainly gotten off the track here. We've gotten into a marshland of perception theory and quantum physics!

> It's all about leading you back to your truth. You can't rediscover your truth, you can't remember your truth, you can't reside in your truth, until you remember *how you get there*.

We are talking here about how you get there.

This dialogue is taking you to where you have always wanted to go: Home. If you can get there before you die, you will never worry again about death. You will never be afraid of dying.

Isn't that what you wish to achieve with this conversation? For yourself and for everyone else?

Yes.

Then our discussion of perception theory and quantum physics has not been a diversion at all—and now perhaps you understand why we are approaching life, and life after "death," from this angle.

Ah! So you are confirming now that there IS "life after death"!

No.

No?

No. There is no life after death.

There is no life after death?

No. In fact, there's no such thing as "death" at all. And that is ...

THE SEVENTH REMEMBRANCE
Death does not exist.

But I know that you *think* that it does, and so, for you, it absolutely does.

That's what we're talking about here.

>We're talking about perceptions, and the perspec-
>tives from which they arise.

Hmmm. So we've come full circle.

>This entire conversation is circular. If you haven't
>already noticed that, you will.
>
>This is not a straight-line dialogue. We are moving in
>swirls here, spiraling back to many important points
>many times. Not just twice, but perhaps three or four
>times. This will be evident to you as our conversation
>continues. And this will not be accidental. This will be a
>quite intentional redundancy.
>
>What is being discussed here is nothing less than the
>cosmology of the cosmos. The secrets of all life. The
>expeditions of the soul after death. The nature of time
>and space. And at least two ideas that will rock the cos-
>mology boat. And sometimes you have to hear things
>more than once to really be able to absorb them. So let's
>move on. We've much to cover. Ready?

Ready.

>So let me repeat here, then, just to be clear, that your
>perspective—that is, how you look at something—
>creates your reality both during this lifetime *and after it.*

So if I don't *think* that there's a life after death, there won't
be one?

>Oh, there will be one, for sure. You can't change
>Ultimate Reality, but you *can* change your experience
>of it. That is why I have said . . .

It is impossible to live or to die without God, but it is not impossible to think that you are.

If you think that you are living or dying without God, you will experience that you are.

You may have this experience as long as you wish. You may end this experience whenever you choose.

All of which leads us to ...

THE EIGHTH REMEMBRANCE
You cannot change Ultimate Reality, but you can change your experience of it.

I'm trying to understand exactly how that works, what that means. I'm looking inside my personal experience to see if I can bring some awareness to that, based on my own walk through life.

Good. That's a very good process. That's a wonderful way to begin. Just don't ever let yourself get stuck there.

What does that mean?

It means, always keep your mind open to things that you may not have personally experienced.

Okay, I've got my mind open.

In this case, let's go back to something that you *can* pull up from your own memory. Talk about taking something from your own "walk through life"—did you ever find yourself out walking when suddenly it began to rain?

Of course. More than once.

> **Good. Now did you experience that moment, the
> reality of that rainfall, as an annoyance and a bother, or
> as a wonder and a delight?**

Well, I can remember, actually, experiencing both. I mean, I remember one time that this happened when I absolutely experienced it as a bother. I was furious that it had started raining. I ran for cover as fast as I could, but it was no use, I got soaked.

Another time I remember walking with a young lady friend of mine on a summer day, and the sky opened. We were in a parking lot with lots of space and the young woman abruptly tore her clothes off and began dancing in the rain! She was dancing and hopping and jumping for joy, and I was standing there dumbfounded, my soaked head of hair falling in streaks across my forehead.

She laughed at me and dared me to join her. So I did. And we danced around that parking lot for almost five minutes before the police came. The officer was very nice—it was a woman, actually—and she simply asked us to put our clothes back on because she did not want to have to arrest us for indecent exposure or becoming a public nuisance. All three of us laughed, and we followed her request, but it was a moment in my life I will never forget. It was sheer, unbridled joy. It was joyful mischief.

> **And, of course, I knew about that moment—which
> is why I used this particular example. Now let me ask
> you a question. What was different about the rain?**

I'm sorry?

In what way was the rain in the first incident different from the rain in the second? Was it wetter? Was it raining harder? Were the water drops colder or bigger?

No. Everything was just about the same, actually. It was no more stormy or furious during the first rain than it was during the second. Both were just nice summer showers.

So what WAS the difference in the two experiences?

The way I looked at them. My perspective. In one instance I had on a business suit and was heading for a very important meeting, and my perspective was that the rain was a nuisance. *More* than a nuisance. It was an intrusion on my plan. It was an obstacle in my way. In the other instance I was dressed quite casually and had no specific time that I needed to be anywhere. It "looked like" the rain could be fun.

Yes. And who created those perspectives?

I did, of course.

You could have decided that the business meeting wasn't that important, or that your showing up a little messed would be completely understood and wouldn't matter, yes? You could have "seen it that way," yes?

Yes.

So now think of the rain as "ultimate reality." You couldn't change the fact that it was raining, but you could change your *experience* of the rain by changing the way you looked at it. You couldn't change Ultimate

Reality, but you could *experience* Ultimate Reality any
way that you wished.

This is the biggest secret of life.

But it isn't always so easy!

It IS always so easy.

But if I changed the way I looked at certain things, then all the
drama would go away.

Ah, *now* we're getting to it . . .

For instance, that Seventh Remembrance—"Death does not
exist." Gosh, if humanity as a whole actually embraced that as
its truth, where would all the drama be? How could we get
angry, or be sad, or mourn the loss of our loved ones? *What would
the Italians do?*

That's very funny.

Do you think Italians will think so?

Of course they will. They'll laugh the loudest.

Okay. But seriously, I mean, really—can this be true? It's one
thing to say that there is life after death, but it's another thing to
say that death itself does not exist. You have said something enor-
mously important here.

You make it sound as if this is something new.
In just about every place I've ever been quoted—no
matter what religion, no matter what culture, no matter what time period or context—I've been correctly
described as declaring that death does not exist—not

in the way that most of you think of it, which is as the end of all life. *There is no such thing* as the "end of life."

So "death" as a human experience does exist.

It is the end of your present physical existence, yes. That experience is over at the time of your death, but life itself is not.

If you have a belief in God, you must have a belief in eternal life, because the gods of all religions declare it.

What if I don't believe in God?

That may change what you experience, but it will not change what is so. What you will experience is what you believe, and what you believe depends on your perspective.

There is no "set way" that it is? There is no one thing that occurs with everyone?

There are "set" things that occur—but you may not know they are occurring.

This is starting to become very confusing.

Sorry. But the truth is that at the moment of death you will experience what you believe, and your belief will be based on what you perceive, and your perception will be based on your perspective.

And is there no chance for my perception to change?

Absolutely there is. Just as in your life before death, your perception can change in your life after death.

What could or would cause that?

A change in your perspective.

Seeing things a new way.

Seeing things a new way.

But what could cause *that?*

A lot of things—including your decision in the moments after your death that the way you are presently seeing things isn't working. That is, that it is not bringing you an experience you choose to have. Such a decision would immediately alter your experience.

Okay, okay . . . suppose that we just . . . is there any way that I can talk you into just describing exactly what occurs at the moment of death, and go on from there?

I would be happy to talk about the *alternatives,* but, as I've said, it will be different for every person.

Give me some of the alternatives, then.

You're asking a very big question. You really want to get into this right now?

Yes. I've waited long enough. I want to know what happens after people die.

Let us be clear. Hell does not exist.
There simply is no such place.

14

I know that this is the Question of the Ages: *What happens following our death?* But I've got to ask it, directly, and I hope you'll give me a direct answer.

> I will. Of course I will. But it's not going to be a short answer. It's not going to be, "Well, you'll either go to heaven or you'll go to hell, depending on what kind of life you've led."
> I can't give you any one-sentence replies to a question like this.

No, you'll have to leave that to the Church.

> No comment.

So . . . your answer?

> Let me begin by saying that there is one thing that *will* be the same for everyone, and that is that your

97

death will be experienced in what you would call stages, or phases, and the first stage is the same for everyone.

In stage one, at the moment of your death, you will instantly experience that life has gone on. This will be the same for everyone. There could be a brief period of disorientation, as you come to realize that you are not with your body, but, instead, are now separate from it.

Soon you will come to understand that while you have "died," you have not ended your life. It is in this moment that you will realize and experience fully, perhaps for the first time, that you are not your body; that a body is something you *can have,* but not something you are. Immediately, you will move into stage two of your death. And this is where individual paths diverge.

In what way?

If the belief system that you embraced before your death includes the certainty of life going on, once you grasp that you have "died," you will know immediately what is happening, and you will understand it. Your second stage will then be the experience of whatever you believe happens after death. This will be instantaneous.

If you believe in reincarnation, for instance, you may experience moments from previous lives of which you have no previous conscious memory.

If you believe that you will be enfolded in the

embracing arms of an unconditionally loving God, that will be your experience.

If you believe in a Day of Judgment or a Time of Reckoning, followed by paradise or damnation for all eternity—

—yes, tell me, what happens then?

Exactly what you expect. As soon as you move through stage one of death and realize that you are no longer living with a body, you will move into stage two and will experience yourself being judged, just exactly as you imagined that you would be, and the judgment will turn out just exactly as you imagined that it would.

If you died thinking that you deserve heaven, you will immediately experience that, and if you think that you deserve hell, you will immediately experience *that*.

Heaven will be exactly as you imagined it would be, as will hell. If you have no idea about the specifics of either, you will make them up right on the spot. Then, these places will be created for you that way, instantly.

You may remain in these experiences as long as you wish.

Well, then, I *can* find myself in hell!

Let us be clear. Hell does not exist. There simply is no such place. Therefore, there is no such place for you to go.

Now . . . can you CREATE a personal "hell" for yourself if you choose to, or if you believe this is what you "deserve"? Yes. So you can send your *self* to "hell," and that "hell" will turn out to be exactly as you imagine or feel a need for it to be—but you will not stay there for one moment longer than you choose to.

Who would choose to stay there at all?

You'd be surprised. A lot of people live within a belief system that says they are sinners and must be punished for their "offenses," and so they will actually stay in their illusion of "hell," thinking that this is what they deserve, that this is what they "have coming" to them, that this is what they *have to do.*

It will not matter, however, because they will not suffer at all. They will simply observe themselves from a detached distance and see what is going on—something like watching an instructional video.

But if there is no suffering, what *is* going on?

Suffering, but there will be none.

I'm sorry?

What is going on is that they will *appear* to be suffering, but the part of them that is watching this will feel nothing. Not even sadness. They will simply be observing.

To use another analogy, it would be a bit like watching your child "play-act" some little scene in your kitchen. The child appears to be "suffering," holding her hand to her head or clutching her stomach, hoping that Mommy will let her stay home from school. Mommy understands perfectly that nothing is really happening. There is no suffering going on.

This is not an exact analogy, but it is close enough to get across the feeling.

So these observers would be watching themselves in this self-created "hell," but they would know that it is not real. And when they have learned what they feel they need to learn (that is, reminded themselves of what they had forgotten), they will "release" themselves and go on to the third stage of death.

What about those who created a "heaven" for themselves? Will they ever go to stage three?

Eventually, yes. They will remember all that they created the experience of their "heaven" to remember, then they will realize the same thing that they realized at the end of their earthly life.

Which is?

That there is nothing more to do.

So they will move on.

They will move on. Into stage three of death. But I don't want to describe that just yet. Let's look at some other "stage two" possibilities for you first.

Oh. Okay. Like what?

You could be one of those who die in a place of uncertainty about whether life goes on at all after death.

Oh, yes, I see. Okay, what happens then?

You will be confused and uncertain as to what is happening, and this will cause you to deal with what is going on in an entirely different way. You will realize that you are not your body, that you are "dead" (this happens to everyone in "stage one"), but since you are uncertain about what, if anything, comes next, you may spend a lot of time trying to figure out how to "proceed."

Will I have help?

All the help you can accept.

In the moments after your "death" you will all find yourself in the presence of the most loving angels and guides and gentle spirits, including the spirit or essence of everyone who has ever been important to you in your life.

My mom? My dad? My brother will be there?

Those you have loved the most will be closest to you. They will surround you.

That's *wonderful.*

The presence of these loved ones and angels will be of enormous help to you, assisting you in becoming "oriented" and understanding exactly what is happening to you, and what your "options" are.

I had heard that we are reunited with our loved ones after death and that they help us "cross over," and I am soooo glad to know that this is true!

> You may even become aware of the presence of some of those loved ones *before* your death.

Before my death?

> Yes. Many people, while they are still in their physical bodies, announce to others in the room that they are seeing loved ones, or that their beloved has come for them.
>
> Those others in the room often try to convince dying people that they are seeing things—and they ARE seeing things, things that are very real, but things that other people cannot see because of their limited perspective. Your perspective widens immensely after "death"—and often in the moments just before you die.

That's exciting! Now you're almost making death sound *exciting.*

> It IS exciting. In fact, your death can be one of the most exciting moments of your life. It all depends on what you believe. As in life, in death what you believe is what you will experience.
>
> For instance, if you do *not* experience the presence of these spirits at the time of your death it will be because you do not expect to, and because the possibility of their presence lies outside of your belief system. Yet if you so much as *hope* that these loving presences will be there, you will immediately perceive them.

I understand. So it is really important to be clear about your beliefs surrounding death.

It is important in life to be clear about your beliefs surrounding *everything*. It is not just your death that is affected by your beliefs, but your *whole life*.

Death is intriguing. It is exciting and intriguing
and totally wonderful.

I have been hearing for a very long time that my beliefs affect my life. I guess I just thought that some sort of *different rules* applied after death. I'm a little surprised to hear that even after death, I'm creating my own reality.

Then I'm glad we're having this conversation.

Wait a minute. What does that say about my father? My father believed that *nothing* happens after death. Absolutely nothing.

If you die in a place of *certainty* that there is NO life after death, once you realize that you have died you will move immediately into stage two, which will be the experience that there is no life.

How can I experience "no life"?

> You will experience nothing at all. There will simply be no experience. Things will still be going on, but you will not be able to perceive them.
>
> It will be exactly as it would be now if you were sleeping while things were going on all around you.

So is there no hope? My father died absolutely certain that there was nothing, no life of any kind, no experience whatsoever, after death ... so ... there's no hope for him ...

> Again, when you die in that place it is like falling asleep. In order to experience something else, you simply have to *wake up*.

How can he wake up?

> The good news is that *everybody* wakes up. Just as in earthly life you would not stay sleeping forever, so, too, will you not remain in oblivious slumber forever in the Afterlife. *That is not the plan.*
>
> The soul will awaken through the ministrations of loved ones and angels. Then it will wonder where it is, why nothing is going on, what has happened. It will begin to put two and two together, and in that moment the soul will move into a conscious awareness of stage two of death.

What will that be like? What did Dad experience?

> What he chose to then experience.

Anything he wished to create? Anything at all?

Absolutely. But if there is confusion, the experience could be a bit confusing. Sort of a mishmash of quickly created scenarios that may or may not make sense.

That doesn't sound very exciting.

Don't worry. It's not a "bad" thing. It's just about getting reoriented. It's like quickly flipping through all the TV channels with a remote. There's nothing harmful going on. You just have to decide which "channel" you want to watch.

If you start to feel a little overwhelmed and begin wishing that you had some help, you will immediately become aware of those loved ones and angels and spirits who have been hovering around you and ministering to you, waiting for you to notice they are there.

In any event, you will soon settle on a picture, from the thousands of pictures in your mind, and you will start creating from there.

But now it is important for you to understand that none of the scenarios that I have just laid out for you have anything to do with Ultimate Reality. That is experienced in the third stage. The scenarios I have just described are the first two stages, the earliest stages, of your "after-death experience."

Okay. So, in the first stage of "death," what occurs is that I will realize that I am no longer my body. In the second stage of "death" I will move through whatever I have imagined or decided will happen when I "die." And in the third stage? Will you describe that for me now? What will happen to me then?

> You will merge with the Essence and begin to experience the Ultimate Reality at the Core of Your Being.

You mean, God?

> You may call the Ultimate Reality anything that you wish. Some people call it the Essence. Some people call it Allah. Some people call it the All. It does not matter what you call it, it is the same thing.

What if that is exactly what I always thought would happen?

> What if *what* is exactly what you always thought would happen?

What if what I always thought would happen immediately after my death was that I would be immersed in God? Wouldn't that then be experienced in the second stage of death?

> Your IDEA about that would be experienced in the second stage, yes. That is because in the second stage of death, you are still operating from your mind.
>
> This would be as pleasant and as glorious an experience as you could make it, in your imagination. But then, in the final stage of death, you would have the experience as it actually is, not as you have imagined that it would be.
>
> But you are right. You are catching on. If what you always believed would happen is that immediately upon dying you will be Home with God, you will be.
>
> This is the world's highest hope, and it is true.

My mother did not hope, she *knew.* My mother *knew* that she would be met by all of the angels, and that she was returning Home.

> And that is exactly what she experienced. Then she moved into the next stage of death, and her imagination turned into an even larger reality.

She experienced the presence of God? You were there to greet her?

> I tell you, I am there to greet *everyone.*
>
> It is impossible to die *without* God. I will always be there.
>
> I will embrace you, comfort you, welcome you, and assure you that you are perfect just the way you are, and perfectly ready to enter into the Kingdom of Heaven. Then I will turn you back over to the souls of your loved ones and to the angels, who will guide you the rest of your way, leading you into the spiritual realm . . . or what you would call "the real" heaven, as opposed to your imagined one. There you will do the work that you went there to do.

I have to "work" in heaven?

> Do not worry. It will be like play. You will be playing in the Gardens of the Gods. It truly will be "heaven." I use the word "work" in the sense of "accomplishing what you set out to do."

And what is it that I will "set out to do" in heaven?

When we get to our explorations of the spiritual realm, we'll take a look at that. Yet know this now: you will not leave my presence until I have made, and you have responded to, the Holy Inquiry.

The Holy Inquiry?

Yes. But I would like to tell you about this later. This might be the most important part of our conversation, and I want to put some building blocks into place first.

Okay . . . but now that's two things you've said are pretty important that you've postponed until later. Earlier you said you had an answer to a question that might really shock me. You said you wanted to lay the "groundwork" for it. Now you're telling me that you're going to reveal to me what "the Holy Inquiry" is, but only after you "put some building blocks into place." So you really have me intrigued here.

Well, death is intriguing. It is exciting and intriguing and totally wonderful.

So if God was there to greet Mom, tell me, what did God look like? I mean, when I meet you, will I be able to recognize you?

What do you want me to look like?

I get to have you look like whatever I want you to look like?

Yes. As in all things, you get to have whatever you choose. Yes, yes, and once more, yes.

If you choose for me to look like Moses, I will look like Moses. If you expect me to look like Jesus, I will look like Jesus. If you wish me to look like Muhammad,

I will look like Muhammad. I will take any form that you expect, or that will make you feel comfortable in My Presence.

What if I don't have any idea about how God looks?

Then I will be a feeling. It will be the most wonderful feeling you ever had. It will feel as if you are immersed in a warm bathing light, as if you are being embraced by love.

Or you may feel as if you are being enveloped in a cocoon, or suspended in a weightless glowing container of absolute, unconditional acceptance. You will experience this same feeling if I should first appear to you in some physical form. Ultimately that form will melt into a feeling, and you will never again have a need to see me in any particular shape or form whatsoever.

Yet now remember what I have said. It is impossible to die without God, but it is not impossible to *think that you are*. You may think anything that you wish in stage two of death. So, the energy of my Pure Essence may surround you and you may choose to dismiss it, downplay the experience, call it an hallucination, or disregard it altogether.

I would never do that. Why would I do that?

You have done it many times during your life. What makes you think you could not do it after your death?

Because I would know better. When I'm dead, I would hope that I would know better. Besides, when I'm dead, you would make it *clear to me* that you are God, and that I am loved, and that this experience I am having is you, welcoming me Home.

> Listen to me.
>
> Death is a moment of creation. There is an energy adjustment at the moment of what you call "death" that fine-tunes *the energy with which you enter into that moment,* producing a duplicating effect in the nonphysical world that you have just entered, so that you may *continue to have the experience you have been creating,* even as you transition into another realm.
>
> (The same process occurs at birth, only in reverse. When you are born, the energy that you have brought with you from the spiritual realm is transformed into matter by this process of energy attunement, producing a duplicating effect in the physical world you have just entered.)
>
> Remember what I said earlier: death is a doorway, and the energy with which you walk through that doorway determines what's on the other side. Now you may *re-create* something new at any moment you choose (just as you may in life), but you will find there, initially, what you *expect* to find there.
>
> If you do not believe in God, and enter into death not believing in God, God will be there and you will not experience God—*any more than you do during your lifetime.*
>
> You have to know that God is present in order to experience God being present.

If you look at a flower and know that God is there, you will see God there. Otherwise, you will see nothing more than a flower. You may even see a weed.

If you look into the eyes of another and know that God is there, you will see God there. Otherwise, you will see nothing more than another human being. You may even see a villain.

If you look into your own eyes in a mirror and know that God is there, you will see God there. Otherwise, you will see nothing more than a person trying to figure out who's there. You may even see a person who does not have the answer to that question.

You mean that God doesn't rescue me from my own "unknowing"?

God is "rescuing" you every day from your own unknowing. Do you know this?

I suppose.

You do?

Well, sometimes.

It is the same immediately after death. Sometimes people know it, and sometimes people don't. And as you believe, so will it be done unto you.

Boy, what a message. I was certainly expecting more than this. I was expecting you to tell me that God's presence in the Afterlife would act as an "override," obliterating all obstructing beliefs and filling the moment with Absolute Glory.

> God will fill the moment with Absolute Glory, for there is nothing more glorious than the Act of Pure Creation, and God will allow you to create in the moment of your death whatever experience you wish.

> This is what happens in stage two of death. In stage three you will come to know a larger Truth about you—and then you will remember again how to create it. For you are a part of the God that you are here talking about. Yet even if you continue to imagine that you are not, you may still create whatever experience you wish.

> And so now, understand this: Your earliest after-death experience is something that you are creating here and now, and that you will continue to create then and there, with your thought about it, and with your hope.

"Hope" plays a role?

> Remember what I told you before. If you so much as hope that someone will come to help you, you will be surrounded by loved ones and angels. If you so much as hope that you will meet Muhammad, Muhammad will guide you. If you so much as hope that Jesus will be there, Jesus will be there. Or Lord Krishna. Or the Buddha. Or just simply the Essence of Pure Love.

> Hope plays a wonderful role in "death" and in "life." (They are the same, of course.) Never give up hope.

Never. Hope is a statement of your highest desire. It is the announcement of your grandest dream. Hope is thought, made Divine.

Oh, what a wonderful statement! *Hope is thought, made Divine.* What a perfectly wonderful statement!

Since you like that statement so much, here is that "100 Word Formula for All of Life" that I promised you.

Oh, yes, one of your delayed promises!

Hope is the doorway to belief, belief is the doorway to knowing, knowing is the doorway to creation, and creation is the doorway to experience.

Experience is the doorway to expression, expression is the doorway to becoming, becoming is the activity of all Life and the only function of God.

What you hope, you will eventually believe, what you believe, you will eventually know, what you know, you will eventually create, what you create, you will eventually experience, what you experience, you will eventually express, what you express, you will eventually become. This is the formula for all of life.

It is as simple as that.

I love when information about life is given to us so succinctly. What a gift! Poets like Robert Frost give us that gift. And songwriters. And playwrights. And authors. And messengers and teachers. I love what another poet, Lisel Mueller, put in a free-verse poem entitled "Hope."

She says that hope "is the motion that runs from the eyes to the tail of a dog." Isn't that great? Doesn't that just capture it? Here's an except from her larger work:

> HOPE...
>
> *... is the motion that runs*
> *from the eyes to the tail of a dog,*
> *it is the mouth that inflates the lungs*
> *of the child that has just been born.*
>
> *It is the singular gift*
> *we cannot destroy in ourselves,*
> *the argument that refutes death,*
> *the genius that invents the future,*
> *all we know of God.*

*You experience a three-dimensional world, but you
do not live in one. Ultimate Reality is far more
complex than you may ever have imagined.*

16

And so again we get back to the idea that the state of mind of
a person at the moment of their death is the experience their soul
will encounter on "the other side."

**Yes, that is exactly what I am saying. I've said it over
and over again here.**

Yes, but I keep revisiting it over and over again because something about that statement just doesn't seem to want to sit well
with me, and I've been trying to figure out what it is. Now I think
I've got it.

Please tell me.

That idea doesn't leave much room for comfort for those who
are approaching death *without* hope—those who find themselves
in a state of fear or terror or apprehension or self-recrimination
or doubt—nor for the families of those who are.

I see. I see where you're going.

Well, I mean, not many people die as peacefully and as wonderfully expectant as you seem to suggest would be necessary for them to have a glorious experience. I would have to think that more people die in . . . what would be the word?—apprehension at least, if not fear or dread or confusion or shock at the suddenness of it, as in an accident, or whatever . . .

I understand your concern. Yet comfort comes in knowing that all souls find peace and joy and love. All souls move to stage three of death, the time of mergence with the Essence.

In the meantime, there is no such thing as "pain"— emotional, physical, or spiritual—in the "afterlife." I mentioned earlier that even those who imagine they are going to "hell" and then send themselves there do not suffer. They simply observe themselves having the experience, but without emotional connection to it.

You said it was something like watching an instructional video.

That's right. That's the level of detachment there is. You simply give yourself the experience in order to review it, pulling from it whatever wisdom there is to extract, but you do not suffer. In life after "death" there is no such thing as suffering.

Then what is there? Is there anything? Is there joy? Is there happiness?

That is all there is. There is nothing negative.

Nothing negative?

   Not a thing.

But I thought you said that persons experience exactly what they expect to experience.

   That is correct.

So what if the person *expects* suffering? What about a person who *chooses* to suffer, who feels that it's the only way they can "earn their way" into heaven, or "pay for their sins"? I thought you said that a soul can experience anything it wants to experience after death.

   What I have said is true. And so you *would* experience suffering . . . except you would not.

Because it's as you said before—you're just watching, and not identifying with the "self" that is experiencing it?

   Yes, and also because, even if you could identify with the part of yourself that is experiencing it, you would not.

You realize that you're leaving me in the dust here . . .

   Let me remind you of something that was said earlier that could explain this all more fully.

Yes, that would be good. Right about now, a fuller explanation would really be good.

   In the moment anything occurs that the soul experiences as not desirable, the very thought that it is not

desirable causes the inner experience of the soul to be instantly altered. And so there is no suffering. Not even for the person who powerfully imagines that he or she *should* be punished.

They would create the experience of their imagining, but they will not experience it as they had imagined, for the simple reason that as soon as they have the experience, they will choose not to.

Even if this is what they really think they want?

The level of awareness in the Afterlife precludes the possibility of anyone willfully choosing what is not real. And the soul would know and understand immediately that the concept and the idea and the experience of "suffering" is not real.

In the first stage of death, the soul comes to understand that the body with which it spent physical life is not real. That is, it is not who the soul really is. In the second stage of death, the soul comes to understand that the mind, with all its thoughts, is not real. That is, it is not who the soul really is.

ALL the thoughts of the limited mind, emerging from the limited perspective of human experience, are impacted greatly in the second stage death, precisely because the *perspective* of the soul in the Afterlife is so much greater than and so different from what it was when the soul was with the body.

It is from the place of this enhanced perspective that the soul begins to create and experience itself. As soon as the soul sees and realizes that it is not a body, its perspective shifts greatly, as you can imagine. This is, in fact, what propels the soul into the third stage of death, when all thoughts—not just "bad" thoughts, but even their own thoughts of "heaven"—are dropped away, and Ultimate Reality is experienced.

And so, even in the case of the person who believes sincerely that he must suffer, that he deserves to suffer, that suffering is the only way to redeem himself in the eyes of his God, the very idea of redemption, and suffering as a means to achieve it, becomes no longer meaningful within the enlarging perspective of the soul.

The soul can *watch* itself *trying* to suffer in its own self-created hell, but the soul will soon come to see that such an experience is not meaningful to create.

I didn't think that anything would be impossible to a soul that is expressing Itself as the Creator of Its Own Reality.

It is not a question of being impossible. It is a question of being meaningless. The soul would have no *reason* to create certain experiences—beyond the fact of the "remembering" that is involved. Once the soul has remembered that suffering is not a reality, but merely an experience created in the human mind, it will have achieved what it sought to achieve with the creation of its own hell, and the experience will thereafter be meaningless.

This is because, in a sense, the soul "knows too much" to get anything more out of such experiences. It would be like a magician performing his own tricks over and over again—for an audience of one: himself.

I should think it would be pretty difficult for a magician to keep himself interested in his own tricks.

> It would be more than difficult. It would be impossible. It is in that sense, in that context, that it could be said to be impossible for the soul to suffer.

But not even for the tiniest moment? Not even while it was deciding to be interested or not?

> No. Not at all.
>
> There is no such thing as "the tiniest moment." Your question resides inside of your reality of what you call "time," where things happen sequentially. Yet all the things that I have described as happening to a soul after death happen at the selfsame instant.

Wait a minute. You, yourself, said they happen in "stages." Stage one, stage two, and so on.

> That is correct, according to your terminology. Yet those stages are experienced simultaneously—with each new experience "erasing" the old. And so it is as if the old never happened. You "are" what you "are" Right Now, and it is very much as if you *never were anything else.*

I'm sorry, that doesn't make any sense. You've just stopped making sense here.

> The challenge here is to speak in earthly terms of a situation or experience that is out of this world. Let me just say that all things happen sequentially and simultaneously.

That makes even *less* sense! Things happen either sequentially OR simultaneously. It can't be both.

> It can't?
> *I am telling you that all of life is both.*

All of life is "sequential" *and* "simultaneous"?

> That is correct.

Well, okay then, this is blowing my mind. I am unable to hold this in my reality.

> Can you conceive of the possibility? Can you stretch
> your mind to be able to conceive of the possibility?
> There is no word for this experience in your lan-
> guage, so we'll have to make one up. Let's say that all of
> life is "sequentaneous." It is "sequential" and "simulta-
> neous" at the same time.

I don't know what to say. I suppose that everything and anything is possible, and I am willing to admit that I don't know everything there is to know about Ultimate Reality, but I can only go so far. Even if I could go there *conceptually*, I can't imagine being there *experientially*. I can't imagine the experience of it.

> Let me see if we can find some other words—some
> "real" words—with which it might be explained to
> you, or made at least a little more clear.

Fine, because I need help here, and I need it immediately. Or should I say, I need it *sequentaneously* . . .

> Perfect. That's perfect!

Now, imagine with me a reality where time does not exist. Not in the way that you imagine. There is only one moment, the Golden Moment of Now.

Everything that has happened, is happening now, and ever will happen—is happening Right Now.

This is true of all of your lifetimes, not just the part of your experience that you call This Particular Lifetime, or the Afterlife. The difference is, in the Afterlife you know it. You experience it.

Okay, but just a second. You just said that *all* of my lifetimes are occurring simultaneously. You mean all of my incarnations, right?

Yes. But I also mean all of your many passages through *this* incarnation.

Do you mean that I pass through *this lifetime* more than *once?*

That is correct. And many possibilities, many experiences, take place simultaneously.

But if everything is happening simultaneously . . . that would mean there would have to be "alternate realities." Are you telling me there are such things as "parallel universes" running alongside ours, in which the "I" that is "me" is having other experiences?

I am.

Well, you told me at the outset that some parts of this conversation might seem "way out" to people, and you're certainly keeping your promise. Lots of folks would say that that last scenario is just plain science fiction.

And it isn't. As I said earlier, this is science.

This, too, is science? Talk of alternate realities is *science?*

Do you think you live in a world of only three dimensions? Ask any quantum physicist about that.

We don't live in a three-dimensional world?

You *experience* a three-dimensional world, but you do not *live* in one.

What does that mean?

It means that Ultimate Reality is far more complex than you may ever have imagined. It means there is more going on here than meets the eye. I tell you that ALL possibilities exist at all times. You are choosing the possibility that you wish now to experience from a multidimensional field of infinite possibilities. And there is another "you" making *different* choices, right here, right now.

Another *me?*

That is correct.

Are you saying that "I" exist multidimensionally?

I am.

There is nothing mysterious about the universe
once you look right at it.

We have once again launched off into a whole different area from that which I thought we were going to explore. Fascinating as this is, is it relevant to my topic—which is life as I am experiencing it, and my death?

> Everything here interlocks. Not a single fact about life and what you call "death" stands alone. All are relevant.

Okay. So then, answer this. If everything is happening at once, how is it possible for the "us" that is "we" to experience events as if they were happening in isolation, sequentially?

> It is a matter of what you choose to look at. And that is an enormously practical piece of information about your present passage through this life.
>
> Your experience is created by what you look at. Or, more correctly, by which way you *move* in Space/Time.

I beg your pardon?

> Let me give you a simple illustration, to see if I can bring you closer to comprehension.

My god, *please.* I'm trying my hardest to track you here, but I need something to hang my hat on.

> Okay. Let us say that you have walked into a room. It is a huge room, and an ornate one. Perhaps it is a library in a richly appointed home.

Fine, I can picture that.

> You walk into the room, and you notice some things "first." Maybe there is a pair of larger-than-life statues of nude human figures in the corner. Naturally, they catch your eye. You move toward them to check them out. Or perhaps there is something else equally dramatic hanging about. A huge stuffed bear. Or a widescreen TV blaring on the side wall. Your attention goes there at once. Your mind goes there immediately.

Okay, I can imagine that.

> Now you begin to look around, and you start to see other things, smaller things, less dramatic things. Finally, you move toward a bookcase in the middle of the room. Your eyes light upon a particular title on the binding of a book in the center of the middle shelf directly in front of you. This is what you came into this room for. The statues caught your eye, and you moved toward them, but this is what you came here for.

Describing this scene to someone else later, you might hear yourself saying, "At last, there it was! Just what I was looking for!"

Of course, there is no "at last" about it. You could just as easily have said, "At first, there it was!"

The coveted book was there all along, waiting for you to see it. It did not show up "later." Indeed, it did not "show up" at all. It did not arrive at a certain "time." It was there all along. Yet you did not see it, because you were not looking at it. You did not move toward it.

Yet everything in that room was there. It all existed simultaneously. You saw what was there, "discovered" it, and therefore experienced it, sequentially. Thus, the moment was truly "sequentaneous."

I get this. I understand how it could have seemed that way.

A thing does not "suddenly appear" when you see it. Your seeing it makes it suddenly "appear" to YOU. Those who dabble in elementary quantum physics would say that nothing is there until you see it. Your seeing it there puts it there. Yet more advanced science now knows that even this is not the ultimate statement of how things are.

In Ultimate Reality, things ARE there before you see them. That is, multiple possibilities exist at all times. Every conceivable outcome of every conceivable situation exists right here, right now—and is *occurring* right here, right now. The fact that you see only one of them does not, in the literal sense, "put it there"—it puts it "here," *in your mind.*

But *which* reality out of the realities that exist is the one that I put in my mind?

> *The one that you choose to see.*

And what makes me choose to see one reality instead of another?

> Well, now, that is the question, isn't it? What *does* make you choose to see one reality rather than another?
>
> When you pass a person spread out on the sidewalk, unkempt, unshaven, gulping a bottle of wine, what makes you choose to see either a "street bum" or a "sidewalk saint"? When you see a written notice from your employer that you have been "downsized," what makes you choose to see either a "horrible disaster" or a "wonderful opportunity"? When you see a television report of an earthquake or a tsunami, with thousands killed, what makes you choose to see either a "calamity" or the playing out of "perfection"?
>
> What *does* make you choose one thing over the other?

My idea about what is there?

> Indeed. Also, your idea about *yourself.*

This reminds me of the story of Don Quixote, the Man of La Mancha, in which one man sees the world through different eyes, eyes that "burn with the fire of inner vision"—as Joe Darion's lyrics in a song from the musical stage play put it. Don Quixote conceives "the strangest project ever imagined . . . to become a knight errant and sally forth into the world, righting all wrongs."

He finds a shaving bowl and, turning it over, sees it as a helmet, wearing it proudly on his head. He encounters a wench of a barmaid, Aldonza, and sees her as Dulcinea, a beautiful damsel, pure and true. He asks her for a token that he might carry into battle, and when she derisively throws him a bar rag, he sees it as her scarf, and carries it next to his heart. He rides off declaring, "I am I, Don Quixote, the Lord of La Mancha. My destiny calls, and I go!"

> And he *made it all up.*
> What, then, is your destiny? How will you live your life? How will you see the people, places, and events in it? And how will it all turn out?

You're God. You tell me.

> *It will depend on how you look at it.*

Do you know what is incredible? As crazy as this is, I think I'm actually understanding this.

> Of course you are, because this is all very natural. Your soul understands all of this—including "sequentaniality"—perfectly. Your soul *knows* that all realities exist. The man on the sidewalk is *both* the street bum *and* the sidewalk saint. Aldonza is *both* the barmaid *and* the beautiful damsel. You are *both* the victim *and* the villain, and have been both in your life. And *none* of it is real. *None of it.* You are making it all up. You create your experience by deciding what part of All That Is you

choose to look at. And you may very well *look right past* something that you were trying to find.

•   Brother, do I get *that*. Some people tell me they are looking for their perfect mate, but when that person is sent to them by the heavens, they don't even see him or her, because they are so distracted by things such as appearances, or what they describe as flaws. Don Quixote saw the barmaid as a beautiful damsel, *and she became one.*

This looking right past something even applies to physical objects. I can't tell you how many times I've gone searching for something that was right in front of my face, but because of one distraction or another I did not look at it. I looked right past it! And so I leave that "room" (that moment in my life) announcing to all concerned, "It's not there. I tell you, it's not there!" Then, much to my dismay, someone else marches into that room and triumphantly returns with exactly what I *swore* was not anywhere to be found!

> This is what a master does. A spiritual master is one who marches into the room of your life and sees what you swear is not there.

So often I've heard people say—heck, so often I've heard *myself* say—"Now, how in the world did *that* get there?"

> Magicians understand this principle perfectly. They say that "the hand is quicker than the eye." They perform their tricks right in front of your face. There is no illusion to it at all. But the magician knows that it will *seem like an illusion* to you because of *where you are looking.*

The secret of the magician's profession is to *keep you looking away from where the trick is being done.*

It is no accident that magicians and spiritual masters have often been thought of in much the same way, and called "mystics." The words *mystical* and *magical* are often put together to describe a particular person or experience.

Mystics are people who see things that you do not see. They are not looking away from the place where the magic is being performed, but rather, right at it.

There is nothing mysterious about the universe once you look right at it, once you see it multidimensionally. This is not easy for most people to do, however, given their limited perspective.

You have placed yourself with a body, inside of Space and Time, seeing, perceiving, and moving in the limited directions of which the body is capable. Yet your body is not Who You Are, but something that you *have*. Time is not something that passes, but something that you pass through, as you would pass through a room. And Space is not really "space" at all, as in "a place where there is nothing," for no such place exists.

Time IS. It is said that "time marches on," but time, in fact, marches nowhere. It is *you* who march on, *you* who "move through time," *you* who create the illusion of "time passing" as you pass through the Only Moment There Is.

And the "Only Moment There Is" is endless, and so, as you move through it, you have the feeling that you are literally "just passing time," *because you are.*

Time is something that you *notice* sequentially while it *exists* simultaneously in all spaces. Space and Time are *sequentaneous.*

As you move down the Corridors of Time, you come to experience that Space/Time is vast. The "Only Moment There Is" is called the Space/Time *CONTIN-UUM* precisely because this space/time reality *continues to always be.*

You, as Pure Spirit, can move through this Singular Reality (sometimes called the Singularity) in endless cycles as you continue to experience your Self. You ARE this Singularity. You are the stuff of which it is made. The Pure Essence. The Energy. You are an *individuation* of this energy and this Essence. You are an "Individuation of the Singularity."

The Singularity is what some of you call God. The Individuation is what some of you call You.

You can split your Self up and move through the Singularity in many different directions. You call these varying movements through the Space/Time Continuum "lifetimes." These are the Cycles of the Self that reveal the Self TO the Self through the Cycling OF the Self THROUGH the Self.

I am floored here. I've never had anyone explain it all to me like this before.

Well, it's about Time.

Oh, now that's cute. You're cute.

Thank you.

So now let me see if I can bring this all down to my individual
Self, and get some perspective on all this. We human beings are
the "individuation of the singularity experiencing life sequentially
simultaneously."

That's it. You've got it exactly right.

Are you kidding me? Did you hear what I just said? I just
SAID . . .

*We are the individuation of the singularity experiencing life sequentially
simultaneously.*

Yes, and I just said you've got it exactly right.

Terrific. I'm in Wonderland here. I've just fallen down the
rabbit hole.

It is your intention to fully know yourself through your experience, not to partially know yourself.

So let me ask you a direct question. This has to do more specifically with life after death.

Okay.

If we are the Eternal Essence, moving through the Singularity that we call Space and Time, on a continuous and *never-ending* Cycle of the Self Through the Self, how, then, do we ever experience eternal life with you—WITH GOD—as we were promised?

Good question.

And your answer?

This continuous Cycle of the Self that you describe IS the eternal life with Me of which you have been told. You are experiencing "eternal life with God" right now.

What, then, is the role of death in all this? And are you saying that this is heaven? Is this ongoing, never-ending Cycle as good as

135

it gets? Do we never experience the "oneness" with you of which
it has been written? What of that moment of Pure Bliss about
which the mystics have sung praises, when the individual soul is
reunited with the All?

> Before our conversation is over, that moment will
> be described for you. Your thirst will be quenched. As
> for your other questions, the movement of the Individ-
> uality through the Singularity never ends, but continues
> in cycles, as has been described.

Cycles that occur sequentially—because a cycle IS sequential
by definition, no? And yet these cycles also occur simultaneously.

> That is correct. Everything is happening at once,
> "seeming" to happen in sequence.
> You use what you call "death" as a means of marking
> the beginning and the end of these sequences, and of
> replenishing your Self between them. "Death" is an
> energy shift that produces enormous fluctuations in
> the rate and frequency of the vibration of your being,
> propelling you back and forth between what you
> would call physical and spiritual life.
> "Death" is not required, however, for you to move
> through the Space/Time Continuum and experience
> your Self at the differing levels.

"Death" is not required?

> Not if you define "death" as the dropping away of
> the physical body. You may have the fullest experience
> of your spiritual self while remaining with your physical

body. It is not necessary to drop away the physical in order to experience that. And you may have the fullest experience of your physical self while journeying within the spiritual realm.

I can take my body with me to the spiritual realm?

You may, indeed.

Then why wouldn't I do this always? Why ever "die"?

Remaining with one physical body through all eternity would not serve the purpose of Eternity Itself.

It wouldn't?

No.

Why not?

Because the purpose of Eternity is to provide you with a Contextual Field of Timelessness within which to offer you an opportunity for Endless Experience and Limitless Variety in the Expression of Who You Are.

You would not plant only one flower in your garden. As beautiful as that flower may be, as glorious as may be its fragrance, it is through variety of expression that the creation you call "flowers" is allowed to *fully flower.*

It is your intention to *fully* know yourself through your experience, not to partially know yourself. To continue to exist with one physical form through all Eternity would not serve that purpose.

Do not worry, however. Changing forms need not produce an experience of loss, because you may

return to any particular physical form at any time that
you wish.

I can come back as who I was before?

Yes, and you frequently do, in order to experience
that particular expression of You in a new and grander
way.

This is described in some of your religious traditions as the second coming of Christ—although many
of you have imagined that this can and will happen for
only one person. The fact is that each of you may experience your Self as the Christed One, and, in fact, all of
you have the potential of doing that at any time.

You may embrace your Sonship at any moment, and
do so in the moment that you realize Who You Really
Are. You will then have fully flowered in the garden of
life. This is the Garden of Paradise, of which you have
written in your mythologies.

Thus do you move through the cycles of life.

These cycles are occurring simultaneously for the
many Individuations that comprise the Singularity,
which is the One Soul.

You may move through Space/Time at several loca-
tions, and, as I said earlier, you may also move through
the *same* location—down the same "time tunnel"—
more than once.

Yes, and you had my head spinning the last time you said this.
Now it's spinning again.

Okay. I think that words are soon going to be failing us completely. Let's see then if a mental picture might help you to conceptualize what we are talking about.

I am about to create a metaphor. This is a metaphor that you may use for the rest of your life. It is important, therefore, to understand that this is not the literal truth, this is a metaphor. This is not how things are, this is a metaphor. Yet metaphors can be extremely useful when "how things are" cannot be explained easily in words that you will understand—or when, indeed, there are *no words for it.*

Metaphors, like parables, can help you to comprehend the incomprehensible. That is why all great teachers have used them.

So let's call this the *Marvelous Metaphor.*

Good. Okay.
Now . . .

You have imagined that there is so much you need
in order to be happy, and even to survive.
You have made this all up.

Create a picture in your mind of a nice, round, juicy red apple. Call this apple "Time," and call the inside of this apple "Space."

It's hard for me to think of the inside of an apple as "space," because there's so much Matter there.

If you saw how much Matter there was in what you call "outer space," you would have no problem at all. Proportionally, the molecules of that imaginary apple are at least as far apart as the solid matter of the cosmos.

Okay...

Now imagine that you are an infinitesimal microbe, small but very much alive, moving through a tunnel in this apple.

> In this metaphor the walls of the "tunnel" are the Corridors of Time. Along the corridor are markings that make each millimeter of wall different from any other. Can you picture this "time tunnel" with its many markings?

Yes, I have a picture of that.

> Good. Now notice as you move through this tunnel that time is not passing. YOU are passing through TIME.

Oh, gosh, I just saw that. You said that before, but I just *saw* that! Boy, a picture *is* worth a thousand words. And what an interesting reversal this picture presents. It's a total conceptual flip.

> Stay with it. Continue to see that Time is not going anywhere. Time is "in place" right *now*. It is static, stable, stationary. It is always there, right where it is. Wherever *you* are in time, it is always Now.
>
> It is you who are on a journey. You are moving through Time.

Okay, I've got it. I'm holding the image. I am moving through Time.

> Now, imagine that the microbe that we are calling "you" is a part of the apple.

I'm sorry?

> Imagine that you are a tiny part, an atom, if you will, of the apple itself. And so, you would be moving through *yourself*, right?

Uh, yes, I guess so. I suppose so.

> You are an atom of this apple, a part of yourself moving through yourself. You could then say that this is atom's apple.

Clever. You are endlessly clever.

> Well, I'm trying to use imagery and words that will help you to form an indelible idea in your mind.

You've accomplished that.

> Good.
>
> Now, you are traveling from the outside to the inside of the apple—from the outermost part to the innermost part of the Self. Can you picture that?

Yes.

> This is your journey through Life. The markings on the tunnel tell you where you are. These markings are actually pictures, and each marks a moment. Every Moment is like a snowflake. There are no two alike in all of Eternity.
>
> You look at the images as you go by. You focus on them, and you move through the tunnel in this way, focusing on one picture after the other. Finally, you get to the Center of the apple. This has been your destination all along. This part of your journey is now over.

I sense this is when I "die." Is this when I "die"?

This is when you "die." You have moved through the physical world and you have reached the Core of this sphere that contains all time and space. You are at "dead center."

Again, clever. And I remain there forever, cuddled in the warmth of the core . . .

No. You have some experiences there (some of which I have already described and more of which I will describe later), then you emerge from it and head toward the opposite outermost part of the Space/Time Continuum—the other side of the sphere.
You have made it to "the other side."

"The other side." Of course. Interesting metaphor. Okay, and what's on "the other side"?

A different reality.

How different?

Entirely different. So different, it would be as if the apple had turned into an orange. This is what we shall call the spiritual realm, and comparing this to the physical world would be—

—don't tell me, I know. It would be *like comparing apples and oranges.* You see? I'm starting to catch onto your Word and Image Games.

Good. That's good. Play with ideas. *Play* with them. Never let them become work. Play with them. And play with life.

And play with each other, while you are at it. Learn to play well. I have sent you to the Garden of the Gods and offered you the whole world in which to play. I have provided sufficient bounty to make certain that there is enough for everyone. No one should go hungry, least of all *die* of hunger. No one need be without clothing to keep warm, nor should anyone be without shelter from the storm. There is enough for everyone.

Beyond that, nothing is needed to play well. Nothing more is required in order to have a glorious experience of Who You Are. You have imagined that there is so much you need in order to be happy, and even to survive. *You have made this all up.*

As you approach your death, you will realize how little any of this matters. *Any of this.* At the moment of your departure from physical life you will know that you have struggled for nothing. And then your long struggle will be over.

You may arrive at this awareness at any time, and end your struggle in any moment. This opportunity and this experience are not held in reserve for only the moment of your death. If you watch closely you will see that each day of your life is crowded with "little deaths." You may use any one of them as a platform for this realization.

Death is a process by which you reestablish your identity.

20

Okay, so we were talking about comparing apples and oranges, and that is how it is now that I have gone, in this metaphor, from the physical world into the spiritual realm, traveling through the Core of My Being in order to get there. When I enter this different reality, when I get to the "other side" of Center, what happens then?

> How you experience what you come to know depends on how you leave Center. If you release your issues and leave them at the Core, then you will feel "centered" because you have not taken your "core issues" with you.
>
> If you do not release them, if you just do not want to let them go, you will take whatever core issues you have not fully released to the "other side," where you will confront them again and have a chance to deal with them there.

If you have ended your own life consciously with the intent to escape these core issues, you will not escape them, but will choose to reverse course and return to the physical world, taking the same Time Tunnel and moving through the same experiences all over again, from the very beginning.

When you refer to "core issues," what you do mean?

Core issues could include the fear of abandonment, or of not being worthy or good enough, or a thought of insufficiency, or an idea of separateness, or any one of a number of false thoughts you may have about yourself.

Ultimately, all core issues have to do with only one issue: your identity. Core Issues may take many different forms, but they all come down to the Only Question There Is: Who Am I?

You are traveling through the Space/Time Continuum to know your Self and to experience this fully—and then to *re-create your Self anew* in the next grandest version of the greatest vision you ever held about Who You Really Are.

Depending upon the nature of the experience you are giving yourself in the physical world, you arrive at the Core of Your Being and venture to the "other side" in one state of being or another.

My experience at the Core does not guarantee that I will know myself fully, releasing any issues I have?

Your experience at the Core WILL be one of knowing yourself fully. Indeed, you will never know yourself *more* fully. Yet, you may or may not choose to release any issues you have. It will all depend on where you wish to go from there. What you wish to Know. What you wish to Experience.

I don't understand.

I shall describe this in much more detail when we talk about the Core Experience itself—the Total Immersion of Self into the Self. For now, know this: You will *emerge from Total Immersion,* and then will come the biggest Moment of Free Choice you can ever imagine.

I will emerge? I won't stay there? I won't remain in Total Immersion with the One?

No.

Do I stay on "the other side," then, for all eternity? Is that where I stay?

No. When you get to "the other side"—when you discover that the "apple" has turned into an "orange" (or, in other words, that you have moved into a whole new reality)—you will realize that you have come there for a reason, for a purpose, and that your work on "the other side" is wondrous work, exciting work, joyful work, but that when it is done, it will be time to journey back.

It is the True Self, the Full Self, that you were introduced to and reminded of at the Core. The conditions on "the other side" are perfect for the work of knowing the Self completely outside of the Core, and in doing this, you make your way along the continuing Corridor of Time to the outer edge of "the other side."

Tell me again, please. What is this "work" my soul will be doing on "the other side"?

It is not work in the sense that it is difficult or arduous. It is, in fact, a great joy. It is the joy of coming to Know what you experienced during your Total Immersion with the Essence as real, as Who You Are. This is "heaven." I will later describe exactly how this work is done.

Immediately following your passing from physical life, when you moved into the third stage of death, hope became reality. Every illusion of physical life was revealed to be just that—an illusion. Your eyes were opened, your perspective was enlarged and enhanced, and, having let go of the thoughts and beliefs held in your mind through the processes encountered at the second stage of death, you began forming new beliefs.

Now remember the Formula for All Life, for it holds true not merely for life in the physical body, but for the Afterlife as well:

Hope is the doorway to belief, belief is the doorway to knowing, knowing is the doorway to creation, and creation is the doorway to experience.

Experience is the doorway to expression, expression is the doorway to becoming, becoming is the activity of all Life and the only function of God.

I don't know why, but I am surprised to hear that there is a place for such things as "hope" and "belief" in the Afterlife.

"Hope" is an energy. Nothing more and nothing less. All thoughts are energies, and what is commonly called the Afterlife is nothing but a field of energy. It is a Cosmic Field of Infinite Possibilities. It is huge, it is vast, but it is quite basic and fundamental in its chemistry, in its energetic elements, in its construction and function. In fact, its elegance lies in its utter simplicity at its basis.

The Afterlife is not a time or a place where souls exist as automatons, having no feelings or emotions. Quite the contrary, it is a place where feelings and emotions run high, creating a contextual field within which souls remember and come to Know once again Who They Really Are.

"Death" is a process by which you reestablish that identity. What you have called "heaven" is the place where you do this. Heaven is not an actual place, but a State of Being. *"The other side" is not a location in the cosmos, it is an expression of the cosmos.* It is a way of being. It is "being in heaven" through the process of self-expression—which is the expression of Divinity Itself, in, as, and through the Self.

Do you understand now?

On "the other side" you move away from the Core of Your Being and into the spiritual realm so that you might better come to Know what you encountered at the Core of Your Being as real, through the perspective of distance, and then to create it IN you, AS you.

Gosh, what *is it* that I encounter at the Core of My Being that is so awesome?

> The True Self, the Full Self. The Glory and the Wonder of Who You Are and of What Life Is.
> In short: God.

Well, what is it like? *What is it like?*

> I will describe this for you later, insofar as it is possible to describe it within the limitations of our present communication.
> For now, it will be most beneficial to continue with our metaphor.

Fine.

> Once at the outer limit of "the other side"—that is, once you have taken what you have come to Know as far as you can go in the realm of Knowing, you—metaphorically—turn around and come back, moving through the spiritual realm once more, this time heading back to the Core of Your Being with all that you Know.
> You are taking your Knowledge back to the Core of Your Being, to now engage in the most sacred process: the re-creation of Self anew, in your next grandest vision, at the Core Level. In your moment of Free Choice, you decide, given all that you know, what you next wish to experience of Who You Are, through the physical expression of it.
> Having once more moved through the experience

of Total Immersion—of being "one with God"—you
are prepared to be born again.

I am going to leave the "orange" and return to the "apple"? I
am going to leave the spiritual and go back to the physical?

Yes.

Why? Why would I want to do that?

In order that you may *experience* what you have
come to *know*. Knowing something and Experiencing it
are two different things.

The process I am here describing is circular.

You enter the Core of Your Being following what
you call "death" in order to reestablish your identity.
You move through the spiritual realm and through that
process come to Know Again who and what you are,
in fullness. You return to the Core of Your Being prior
to what you call "birth" to *re-create* your identity anew,
in the next grandest version of the greatest vision ever
you held about Who You Are. That is, you elevate your
experience and expression of Self, moving it to the
next level. This is called evolution. You live your life in
the physical world, that you might Know your Self in
your own Experience. Reentry into physical life—an
extremely "heavy," dense existence compared to what
you have just embraced—produces a loss of the full
identity you have established. This is by design. Were
you to know the fullness of it, you could not experience it in any of its parts—and that is precisely what
you have come to the physical world to do. When this

"work" is done (it is intended to be a totally joyful experience, as is your experience in the Afterlife), you "die again," once more entering the Core of Your Being in order to reestablish the fullness of your identity. You reemerge and move through the spiritual realm to express who and what you are in fullness through Knowing. You return to the Core of Your Being prior to what you call "birth" to *re-create* your identity anew, in the next grandest version of it. You give your self birth and live your life in the physical world, that you might Know your Self in your own Experience. When this "work" is done, you "die again," once more entering the Core of Your Being in order to reestablish the fullness of your identity. You move through the spiritual realm and through that process come to Know Again in fullness who and what you are. You return to the Core of Your Being prior to what you call "birth" to *re-create* your identity anew, in its next grandest version. You give your self birth and live your life in the physical world, that you might Know your Self in your own Experience. When this "work" is done, you "die again," once more entering the Core of Your Being in order to reestablish the fullness of your identity. You move through the spiritual realm and through that process come to Know Again who and what you are. You return to the Core of Your Being prior to what you call "birth" to *re-create* your identity anew, in its next grandest version.

The process continues.

Eternally.

Total Immersion with the Essence at the Core of Your Being produces the energy attenuation (what you would call the vibrational adjustment, or "quickening of the spirit") making possible subsequent reemergence into either the spiritual realm or the physical world.

The Cycle of Life continues eternally because it is the desire of All That Is to Know Itself in Its Own Experience.

This is, in fact ...

THE NINTH REMEMBRANCE

It is the desire of All That Is to Know Itself in Its Own Experience. This is the reason for all of Life.

Remember that I have told you, a soul arrives at Complete Knowing along the path of the spiritual world, and at Complete Experiencing along the path of the physical world. Both paths are used, and that is why there are two worlds. Put them together, united at the Core, and you have the perfect environment within which to create Complete Feeling, which produces Absolute Awareness.

Remember that I told you, the Moment of Absolute Awareness—that is, of Knowing and Experiencing and Feeling Completely Who You Really Are—is arrived at in steps. Each passage through a lifetime can be considered one of those steps.

So I return to the physical in order that I might gain "a world of experience"!

Exactly. You have put it very well.

Before you make this return journey to physicality, you first merge again with the very Essence of the Self at the Core of Your Being. You merge, and then you emerge, to journey onward to the outermost edge whence you came.

May I ask a question here? What happens when I finish all the steps—we'll call them lifetimes—and arrive, at last, at Absolute Awareness? Do I then finally get to remain in "heaven"? Do I stay inside the Core? Do I experience Total Immersion eternally?

You would not choose to.

Why not?

If you fully self-realized, your grandest desire would be to experience that as a discrete physical reality.

And—?

And you would return to the physical world.

Right back to where I came from.

Right back to where you came from.

In the same body experiencing the same life over again, or in a different body experiencing a different life?

It would be as you wish. You would decide this when you arrive at the biggest Moment of Free Choice you could ever imagine.

Some souls that have achieved mastery have chosen

to return to experience this in the same body in which they took their last steps on the path. Others have chosen to return to physicality in an entirely different body, living an entirely different life.

Either way, you would now Know fully Who You Really Are. You would be living in Absolute Awareness. So absolute would be your awareness, so complete would be your Knowing and Experiencing, that others would know and experience Who You Are as well, and they would call you Rabbi, and Master, and Teacher.

They might even swear that I am "The One."

Yes. And they might think that there is no other like you. Then it would be your job to convince them that this is inaccurate, and that *every one of them* is like you, and that they can all know and experience all that you know and experience.

What you Know and Experience would be your greatest joy, and you would seek to share it with everyone. And you would think nothing of giving up your physical life if doing so meant that you could show others who they really are.

It might look as if other people are taking your life, but you would know exactly what is happening. You would know that no one "dies" against his will, neither at a time nor in a way that is not of his choosing. And so you would use your "death" as a moment of creation, producing in many others an opening to a Much Larger Reality.

Well then, either way—whether I arrive at Absolute Awareness or continue on with my journey there—it is true that eventually I would find myself at the outer edge of the "apple," where I began, yes?

Yes. You will have come full circle.

And are you going to tell me that I will then turn around and go through the whole cycle again? And keep on going back and forth over and over and over?

You may, if you choose.

So I really *could* be living the *same lifetime,* over and over again?

We have a lot to talk about here . . .

You can say that again.

*Not all things are the way they seem. There are more
possibilities in every moment within every lifetime
than you might previously have imagined.*

Look, I've heard about how we all live many *different* lifetimes—but you have told me here several times now that we are all also living the *same* lifetime over and over, like some real-life version of that movie *Groundhog Day*.

This is a great deal for you to grasp, especially in one sitting, so perhaps we should move a little more slowly here.

You are asking deep and important questions about "life," "death," and "dying," and in order to fully understand what you are *calling* "death" and "dying," it is necessary to explore some very esoteric topics of what might be termed "the cosmology of everything." But let's go a little more slowly.

Okay. I do feel as if we have been racing. I mean, I've been given more data in the last ten minutes . . .

I know. So let's double back here just a bit and pick up some of that data and look at it again.

I have said that you are a part of All That Is. You are—to return to our metaphor—an atom of the apple+orange, and you are traveling through it.

We could call this the *Applorange!*

That's good. That will make this metaphorical image unforgettable. We'll use your coined word to refer in shorthand to the Space/Time Continuum.

Okay, good.

Now, you may travel through the *Applorange* repeatedly, along any route you choose. As I said, this could be the same route that you chose before, or it could be another route, another "tunnel."

And you may also choose from any number of different *ways* of moving through the Corridor of Time, changing your movements from moment to moment if you wish.

What do you mean?

Well, you tell me how you might see yourself moving through the Corridor of Time. Let us say that you are suspended in midair in that corridor. You are, quite literally, "suspended in time." Now, which way might you see yourself moving?

Forward. I see myself moving forward through the tunnel. Is that what you're asking me?

Is there any other way you might move?

Well, *backward*, I suppose. Are you saying that we can move backward in time?

Ah, here you are touching on something that is very significant. More significant than you might know right now. That is part of the Holy Inquiry, of which I spoke earlier.

Ah, are you going to tell me what the Holy Inquiry is now?

Not just yet, but soon. I have a few more building blocks to put in place. The shorthand answer to your other question is, yes, you can move "backward in time," not just to other lifetimes, but *within* any particular lifetime.

Fascinating.

But can you think of any other direction you could move in that tunnel?

Uh, no. Backward and forward would be it. Well, maybe side to side.

That's correct. If you were suspended in the Corridor of Time, you could also move left to right. Is there any other way?

Up and down?

Correct. You could move up and down. And so, there are three ways you see that you could move—back and forth, left and right, up and down. Can you think of any other way you could move?

Hello?

I'm thinking.

No, I guess not.

Most people cannot.

Why not?

Because they experience themselves as part of a three-dimensional environment. But what if I told you there is a fourth spatial dimension inside that tunnel, a fourth direction in which you could move?

I would be bewildered. I can't guess what it is.

You could move *circumferentially*. From your suspended position inside the Corridor of Time, you could move in a clockwise or counterclockwise direction.

I didn't think of that.

The tunnel has three distances ... the distance from beginning to end (forward/backward), the distance from side to side (left/right), and the distance top to bottom (up/down). It also has a fourth distance—the distance *around* its interior space (circumference). This is the Fourth Dimension in Time ... and so there are more ways of "moving through time" than you might previously have imagined.

You're right. I just never thought of this fourth way.

Actually, in the Space/Time Continuum there are more spatial dimensions than four.

More than *four?* Good heavens, how many?

The number really does not matter here. If you wish to know more about this at the technical level, talk to a quantum physicist. Again, this is simply today's science. All that matters for the purpose of this discussion is for you to know and understand that not all things are the way they seem, that there are more possibilities in every moment within every lifetime than you might previously have imagined.

Still, your journey is the same, in the sense that the destination is the same. It is your route that may have more possibilities for variation than you thought.

What would determine which choice I make, given all these options?

It has to do with what you wish to experience. All paths may lead to the same destination, but each "route" offers different experiences. Since you are making continuous journeys through the Space/Time Continuum, endless in number, taking any route that you wish, there is no "risk" of "losing a chance" to take any particular route, so your options are wide open.

And this goes on forever? I never get to stay in the spiritual life for all eternity?

You remain nowhere for all eternity.

Not even in the Center, in the Core of My Being? I know I asked this before, but . . .

Go on.

I remain nowhere for all eternity?

> You must put a space in that word "nowhere," as I have taught you before, in order to understand the statement.
>
> The word "nowhere" with a space in the middle reveals: "now here."
>
> You remain *Now Here* for all eternity.
>
> "Now Here" is the only Time and Space there is.

This really is mind-expanding. So, heaven, "paradise," nirvana, reunion in bliss with God, is *not* at the Core?

> Yes, it is—but it is also *everywhere else*. It is not a case of it being "here" and not "there." It is everywhere.
>
> Yet there is something unique about the Core that you find in no other place within the Space/Time Continuum—and that is why you go there.

What is it?

> The Singularity.
>
> At the Core of Your Being, All That Is and All That You Are appears in its Singular Form. It is here that Knowing and Experiencing merge.
>
> This merging may be created by you at any time and place within the Continuum, but at the Core of Your Being there is nothing else to "compete" with it, nothing else to take your attention from it. It is all that there is.

Okay, well then, *that's heaven. That's where I want to stay.*

No, you don't. That's what you want to Know and Experience, but that's not where you want to stay.

Why *not?* Sure sounds good to me!

If you Knew and Experienced IT and NOTHING ELSE, you would ultimately lose yourself in the mergence. You would no longer know you were *having* the mergence, because there would be no *other* Knowing or Experiencing with which to compare it. You would not even know who you are. You would lose your ability to differentiate, to individuate your Self.

Are you actually telling me that "heaven" could get to be "too much of a good thing"?

I am telling you that all things exist in the Space/Time Continuum in perfect balance. The Essence of Who You Are knows precisely and exactly when the Process of Life Itself calls for you to merge with the Oneness and to emerge from it, in order for you to Know the bliss of the Oneness through the Experience and the glory of its Individuation.

The system works perfectly. The balance is precise. The design carries the elegance of a snowflake.

To the Oneness you return, and from the Oneness you emerge, over and over again, eternally and forever, and even forevermore.

And this is ...

THE TENTH REMEMBRANCE
Life is eternal.

Yes, well, every religion tells us that. Every faith tradition on the earth proclaims it. And now here we are again, hearing that.

It is true that I have been sending this message to you through many messengers over many centuries.

Rossiter W. Raymond was a writer, editor, orator, theologian, teacher, novelist, consulting mining engineer, and practicing lawyer who lived from 1840 to 1918, and his most famous quote was:

Life is eternal; and love is immortal; and death is only a horizon; and a horizon is nothing save the limit of our sight.

I suppose he was one of your messengers.

He was.

And contemporary entertainers are, too, I guess. Like Carly Simon. She used the Raymond quote when she recorded a song written with Teese Gohl a few years ago to send a message to a new and wider audience about being Home with God. And Alanis Morissette. She has been saying *a lot* lately about life and the nature of existence through her music. And filmmaker Stephen Simon through his movies, and now his Spiritual Cinema Circle. And . . .

Let me make something clear here. You are *all* my messengers. Every *one* of you.

You are all sending a message *to* life *about* life through your own life, lived.

The question is not, "Are you a messenger?" The question is, "What is the message you are sending?"

There is no such thing as the truth.

22

The Tenth Remembrance does not surprise me even a little, nor does it take my breath away with its originality.

> I'm sure it doesn't. But it *should* take your breath away with its meaningfulness. There will be nothing more meaningful said in this entire conversation.
>
> When you know that life is eternal you never again fear "death," because you see and understand the nature of it, the wonder of it, the glory of it, the perfection of it, and the impeccable gift that it is.

Maybe one day I may write a separate book: *Death, the Impeccable Gift.*

> That would be a very good book. A small handbook. A little "instruction book" for the dying and their loved ones. That would be an extraordinary contribution.
>
> In the meantime, we have this conversation to complete, so that you and others who are exploring these

subjects more deeply may more deeply understand them.

The question now is not whether, when you have finished this conversation, you will understand what you have always wanted to understand, but whether you will believe what you will have come to know.

Why would I not believe it?

Because humanity has always had the most difficult time believing the most wonderful truths, and the truths about "death" are the most wonderful truths of all.

These are wonderful truths, I must admit. I want so much to believe every word here. I just hope they *are* true.

You see? There you are already, questioning them. Oh, ye of little faith . . . do you not see that when you are questioning them, you are questioning your Self?

If you love the truths that you find in your soul, do not abandon them because someone outside of your soul does not agree with them or ridicules or questions them. You are not saying that your truth is THE truth. You are saying that it is YOUR truth.

There is no such thing as THE truth. We've already gone over that. Let it be enough that you get in touch with YOUR truth.

This is my truth. What I am coming to understand through my conversations with you is my truth.

> That is sufficient. That is enough. In fact, that is more
> than enough. That is very powerful. Do you know how
> powerful it is to have gotten in touch with your own
> truth—about *anything*?
>
> Others will get in touch with their truth as a result of
> this conversation as well. Because, "in truth," this is not
> just your conversation, it is theirs also. Everyone who is
> reading these words has created this conversation. Do
> you know that? Do you know that, *as you are reading
> these words,* you are creating where they are going next?

That is a mind-boggling concept. It is hard to get my head
around, because the end of this book already exists. We could flip
to the end right now and see what it says. So if all of us reading
this are creating it as we go, how come the end already exists?

> The book on the shelf of the richly appointed
> library already existed, too, but it did not exist in your
> reality until you *saw it there.* EVERYTHING that you
> have created is already there. *Everything.* The fact that it
> is already there does not mean that you have not cre-
> ated it. It simply means that you are not *aware* that you
> have created it, because from where you are now in
> the Space/Time Continuum you cannot see *that.*

Do you know just how mind-bending all this stuff really is?

> I think I have a pretty good idea.

I am so happy now. I feel as though I'm being given the information behind the cosmology of the universe. This is the *mechanism*
of life and death. So I suppose now I can go ahead and die . . .

> You will choose to "die" when your life on earth is complete. Your life on earth will be complete when you have experienced *all* that you came here to experience.

Or when I realize that I have not experienced all of it and that there is no other way to experience all of it along the path I have taken.

> No. Emphatically, no. That cannot happen. No one dies having failed to experience all that they came to the physical world to experience.

What?

> I said that *no one dies having failed to experience all that they came to the physical world to experience.*
> There is no such thing as being "incomplete."
> That is what is meant by . . .

THE ELEVENTH REMEMBRANCE
The timing and the circumstances of death are always perfect.

I believe that. But how does the parent of a child who has been raped, mutilated, and murdered call the circumstances of such a death "perfect"? How do people who saw their loved one perish on 9/11 accept such a death as "perfect"?

You are asking an awful lot here. This is stretching the credulity of most people to the absolute limit.

> I have already said that the elegance of life's design is like that of a snowflake. It seems almost too perfect to be believed, too good to be true. Yet I tell you this:

Comfort for the bereaved will be found in the sure knowledge of the certain perfection of God.

God is perfect, always and eternally. Now there is only one thing left for you to understand: who and what "God" is.

I have told you over and over again in our conversations, and I will tell you here and now, once more, and finally:

GOD and LIFE are one and the same.

Therefore when I say that "God is perfect," I am saying that Life is perfect. And it is. The "system" rests in perfect balance with itself.

All things happen in their perfect timing and in their perfect way. It is not always possible to see this, to perceive this, from the extremely narrow perspective of human experience. That is a limitation of the physical world. It is a limitation that can, however, be overcome.

Many "prophets" and "sages" have overcome this limitation of perception by choosing a different perspective, by looking at life a new way. Alas, their messages are often ignored. Their insights are frequently belittled. Often, they themselves are condemned. And so the blind continue to lead the blind, because you will not listen to those who can see.

Therefore, let those who have ears to hear, listen: Imperfection is impossible in the Kingdom of God.

Yes, but what about here on earth?

"Here on earth" IS the Kingdom of God. There is no place that exists that is not part of that kingdom.

You see, we have this all "separated out" here on earth. We've got it that life on earth is the trial and the tribulation *enabling us to get INTO* the Kingdom of God. And it's our idea that death is the way we get in.

> There is no way to get into the Kingdom of God. It is not a place you get into or out of. It is a place where you always ARE. It is the only place that you can ever be.

It sure doesn't seem that way sometimes.

> That is because you do not remember who you are, and you do not treat others as who they are. If you did, you would experience heaven on earth. You would be Home with God *everywhere*. And *always*.

Is there any way that people will ever, *can ever,* "get" that?

> Conversations such as this are one way. Do not keep this conversation to yourself. Make sure it gets into as many hands as possible. Share it with the world.
> But first, bring the meaning of this message deeply into your own life. See God in everyone and everything, and see everything as perfect.

You mentioned this earlier, when we talked about people feeling victimized. You suggested that we change our perspective and see everything as perfect even when, in human terms, it is obviously not.

> Perhaps especially when it's not. For such awareness will bring you peace in the midst of turmoil, rest in the

space of weariness, forgiveness in the moment when resentment and anger might appear, and a greater love for life than you have ever experienced before.

Search for the perfection in every moment. *Search* for it. Diligently. Faithfully. *Know* that it is there, and that you will find it if you will but look deeply.

Now, do you remember when I said, quite early in this conversation, that we would have another opportunity to explore this idea of "perfection," and that I was going to ask YOU to give ME an example of that? Well, I am going to ask you now to tell the story of Billy, from your workshop.

I knew it. I knew then that this is what you were going to bring up. It's the first thing I thought of when you started talking about this.

Good. So tell the story.

Sure.

"Helen" was one of ninety-seven participants at one of my ReCreating Yourself retreats, held during the week between Christmas and New Year's every year for the past ten years. On the final night of the retreat before our New Year's Eve resolutions ritual, Helen raised her hand and asked for the microphone.

"I've heard a lot this week about how God is our best friend, how God is wonderful and loving, and how we should all have a conversation with God every day," she began. "Well, if I had a conversation with God, I would tell Him that I am damned angry with Him."

"That's okay," I said. "God can handle that. But are you okay?"

"No," she said, and her voice was trembling now.

"Well, just what are you so angry with God about?"

Helen took a deep breath. "Almost twenty-one years ago we adopted a baby boy. We had tried to conceive for five years, without success. It looked like we would never be parents. My biological clock was running out. So we adopted Billy.

"Three weeks later, I discovered I was pregnant. I had the child, another boy, and raised them both as my own, although we did tell our first son when he grew a little older that he was adopted. We wanted to be truthful with him. We told him we loved him exactly the same as his brother, and we knew that our actions showed him that.

"Billy was eight. He must have innocently shared this information with some of the children at school, because one day he came home from school very angry. He had been teased on the playground about not having any mommy. You know how kids can be. They can sometimes be very cruel. They were saying things like, 'Billy's so ugly that even his mom didn't want him.' Anyway, he came home so hurt and just furious, wanting to know why his mommy would give him away—and demanding to know who she was and to see her right away.

"I felt terrible, of course. First, for the anguish and hurt that I could see Billy was going through, and second for myself. I was filled with sadness because, of course, I felt that I was Billy's mommy. I stood there remembering the nights of changing diapers and nursing him through sickness and all the things that mommies do, and my heart broke that Billy didn't see me as 'Mom' anymore, didn't think of me that way.

"But I understood—I had to understand—and I promised him that when he was older, if he still felt he wanted to, he would meet his mom. I would do whatever I could to find her and arrange it.

"This seemed okay with Billy, but he never did get over his anger. He just had this anger all through the rest of his childhood and into his teen years, which were very difficult for us. We all got through it, but it wasn't easy on any of us in the family, and certainly not on me.

"When Billy had grown older, we talked again about seeing his mother, and we made an agreement that when he turned eighteen I would begin searching for her if he still wanted me to. Throughout the rest of his teen years he reminded me of that promise.

"Finally, Billy's eighteenth birthday arrived. That day he was killed in a motorcycle accident."

There was a collective gasp from the retreat participants. Abruptly, Helen's energy shifted into anger.

"Now I want *you* to tell *me*," she snapped, "how any kind of loving God could have let that happen, just when Billy was about to meet his mother, just when his father and I were about to reconcile the strain that his yearning had placed on our relationship. I want you to tell me, *why would God do that?*"

The room plummeted into stunned silence. I was stopped cold. I stared at Helen for a moment, then closed my eyes and went within. I heard my thoughts. "Okay, God, this is it. I don't know what to say here. You've got to help me out."

Suddenly, my eyes popped open, my mind overflowing. I spoke the words I heard in my head before I had a chance to judge them or edit them.

"Billy died on that day because that was the day on which he was promised he would meet his mother—and he did. On that day his mother was not on this earth."

The room gasped again. Someone whispered an emphatic *"Yes."* Someone else openly cried.

I went on.

"There is no such thing as an accident, and nothing happens by coincidence. You were given a biological son, even though you had not been able to conceive and it looked as if you might never be able to do so, because there was a plan—a larger plan— in place. You were given this special gift of your biological son in exchange for your willingness to take Billy in, give him a home, love him and raise him as your own, and care for him until he was ready to meet his mother and she was ready to meet him.

"The day of Billy's death was the happiest day of his life. His gratefulness to you for bringing him to that moment is eternal. It surrounds your heart even now, and creates with you an everlasting bond.

"There is perfection in Life's design. In every human circumstance and experience. In every condition. Our opportunity is to notice this. That is also our release. Our salvation. The end to our suffering and our pain."

Helen's face changed immediately. Filled with anger just moments before, now it was aglow. Her whole body seemed drained of every tension. She looked relaxed for the first time in a very long while. Tears ran down her cheeks even as she smiled with a radiance that filled the room.

I've told this story because I want everyone to know what Helen and all the other participants in that retreat now know. There is a "magic formula" that has been given to us by the heavens. It is a formula with which all sadness, all anger, all negativity surrounding any human experience is dissolved. It is a formula that allows us to re-create ourselves anew. It is a formula easy to remember, and stated in three words:

SEE THE PERFECTION.

Ah, but does it work? Does it really work?

On New Year's Eve, Helen handed me a note that she'd written when she'd returned to her room after a walk under the clear, crisp Colorado sky the night before. Like Robert Frost and Lisel Mueller, she had also turned to poetry to speak the beauty of her knowing.

> I came here with a burdened heart,
> A heart afraid to cry.
> It's near three years since Billy left
> And I couldn't say goodbye.
> I stood, alone, beside his grave
> And couldn't even cry.
>
> We had a deal, I said to him
> You left me high and dry.
> It's near three years since Billy left,
> God had not seen fit to try
> To soothe this hurt, to heal this heart,
> To give me tears to cry.
>
> And then God spoke, He pointed out
> That even though He tried,
> My heart was closed and couldn't hear
> His gentle, ageless sigh.
> And though it was just Neale whose voice
> Brought the message from on high,

My spirit heard God's words tonight,
And now my eyes can cry.

I took a walk this starry night.
It's finally time to try
To find the joy to free my son.
It's time to say goodbye.
And as I did, a shooting star . . .
. . . danced across the sky.

No death is wasted, and all death
brings a message to those who leave the earth
and to those who remain.

That is a wonderful story. It illustrates perfectly how each journey through the Space/Time Continuum is designed to bring every soul a special experience, and how the timing and the circumstance of every "death" is always perfect.

I certainly do see how it was "perfect" that this young man left his body when he did, because he said he wanted to meet and know his biological mother, and he was given his wish through the device of his death.

What I don't see is how it was "perfect" that it all had to happen this way—and I certainly don't see how this young man had the "special experience" that he came here to experience.

Billy came here to experience being frustrated all of his life and then having to die in a motorcycle accident just to finally meet his mother? *Come on!*

Do not presume that you can know, or can surmise from the "facts," what is the path of the soul. You cannot know of the delicate interweavings co-created by all of the Blessed Beings involved in the life experience just related. Billy came here to serve ALL agendas.

All agendas?

There were many souls interacting and co-creating here, as there are in every moment of life, everywhere. In this case those souls included the young man on the motorcycle, his biological mother, his adoptive mother, his adoptive father, and his brother—as well as the soul of the person driving the vehicle that hit and killed him.

And this says nothing about other souls, some of them more removed, such as the young man's biological father, the friends and relatives of all of these people, and—are you ready for this?—YOU, and *the people in your workshop.*

Each has an agenda that is being served.

And so, with this understanding, we come to . . .

THE TWELFTH REMEMBRANCE
The death of every person always serves the agenda of every other person who is aware of it. <u>That is why they are aware of it.</u> Therefore, no death (and no life) is ever "wasted." No one ever dies "in vain."

This places personal tragedies and national disasters and mass casualty tolls and the death of every individual into an entirely different context. Suddenly, everything from the crib death of a single baby to the annihilation of thousands can be understood in a whole new way.

Yes.

When you understand the endless and miraculous interweavings of life, every death is transformed into an event of enormous celestial significance.

The deaths of 9/11 and the deaths of the tsunami of 2004 and the hurricanes of 2005 and the deaths of the genocide in Darfur and the deaths of the Holocaust are all elevated to a place of honor.

The deaths of grandmas lying in sickbeds for years and the deaths of children darting into unsuspecting traffic and the deaths of AIDS patients and the deaths of test pilots and the deaths of people who died in peace and who died in violence, heroic deaths and deaths that go unnoticed—*all deaths* are elevated to the level of extraordinary meaningfulness, for every life touches thousands, and every death redeems them.

All death is redemptive because all death returns each soul to the truth of itself, to the truth of life, to the truth of God—and every person who is touched by any death is opened to this truth, and so, may experience it as well.

I tell you, no death is wasted, and all death brings a message to those who leave the earth and to those who remain. It is for you to seek that message and to find it, to hear it, and to heed it.

What *is* the message of the Holocaust? What *is* the

message of 9/11? What *is* the message of the tsunami and the crib death and the AIDS patient and the loving grandparent who slips away in the middle of the night?

Indeed, what is the message and the purpose of *all death and of all of life?*

Will you tell us? Can you tell us here?

The message is what you announce it to be. The purpose is what you demonstrate it to be. You do the announcing and the demonstrating through the living of your life.

You are both the message and the messenger. You are both the creator and the created. You are in the process of producing the message even as you are delivering it. Indeed, the process of delivering it IS the process of producing it. They are one and the same.

Think on this. Think on this deeply.

This much I can say to you: Life Itself is a glory and a wonder far beyond anything you have previously imagined—and you, yourself, are a glory and a wonder far beyond anything you have previously experienced.

This life, which you live—this life, which you *are*—is everlasting and eternal. It never ends, *ever.*

All souls are interacting and co-creating in every moment. All souls. There is an interweaving going on. An interweaving that produces the breathtaking tapestry of life. Each thread takes its path, but to assume that each thread is therefore "on its own" would be to vastly misunderstand how the Larger Picture is created.

My God . . .

    Your God, indeed.

So life is not a singular experience.

    Actually, it IS.

    It is the experience of the Singularity, knowing Itself as Itself through the experiences of its Individuations. There is but a Single Agenda, and it is served through the distinctly different but remarkably co-joined experiences of every one of us.

    That Single Agenda is for Divinity to be expressed and experienced in all its splendor, and to re-create and define Itself anew in every single golden moment of Now. HOW it expresses itself, HOW it experiences itself, HOW it defines itself, is up to you. That is the decision you are making every day. That is the choice you are demonstrating every moment. You are doing so individually and collectively. Every act is an act of self-definition.

    Of this truth, and many others, you will be reminded when you merge with the Core of Your Being. It is here that you will be rejuvenated, reunited, and reintegrated, should you have forgotten the original agenda, should you have lost your memory and your sense of Who You Really Are. And if you have not, but rather, have a full awareness of all of this and a full experience of it, it is at the Core of Your Being where you will be replenished.

    The great misunderstanding of all those who have forgotten the Ultimate Truth, the great illusion of all those who live in temporary amnesia, is that there is somewhere they have to "go," somewhere they have to journey, in order to "get to heaven," or "unite with God," and experience eternal bliss.

There is nowhere you have to go, nothing you have to do, and nothing you have to be except exactly what you are being right now, in order to experience the bliss of the Divine.

You ARE the bliss of the Divine, and you simply do not know it.

Then why bother taking these endless trips through the *Applorange?* Why am I continuously journeying through the Space/Time Continuum? Why have I undertaken this endless search for God?

Your journey is not an endless SEARCH for God, it is an endless EXPERIENCE of God.

Understood in this way, the reason for the continuous journey becomes apparent. The journey is a process. It is the way that you know God—indeed, that you know yourself AS that which is Divine. This journey is therefore your greatest joy.

Okay, so I am taking these "trips" through time and space in order to experience God. But when do I actually meet God? Earlier you said that God will be the first experience I will have after my death.

If you believe that it will be, then it will be. But you do not have to wait until then. In fact, *you have been meeting God all along. That is what I have been telling you.*

Here is the central error of most human theology: You think that one day you are going to meet God. You imagine that you are one day going to get back Home. You are *not* going to get back Home.

You *never left Home*.

The entire universe is composed of one thing,
acting differently. . . . You are experiencing your Self
as the Multitudinous Individuality.

W ell, you said you were going to circle back on major points
several times, and you have. And what you are laying out for us here
is a whole new spirituality. It is a new way of looking at things.

I used to think that I was outside of the apple, wanting and
hoping to get a taste of it. That's what the old spirituality taught
me. But you are saying that I am *not* outside the apple, but a *part*
of the apple, moving *through* the apple, and the *entire apple* is God.
God is not only at the core, at the center of all things, God IS all
things.

That is correct.

Now you are using the metaphor to see past the
metaphor.

You have been imagining that you stand outside of
God, but you do not stand outside of God. You CAN
not. God is All There Is. It is impossible for anything to
exist outside of All There Is.

And so, I am—

—that is correct. Just as you have already stated, you are a part of the *Applorange* moving through the *Applorange*. You are a part of God, getting a taste of God.

And just how am I doing that? I mean, how is my endless, cyclical movement through the Corridors of Time giving me a "taste of God"?

By giving you the endless experience of yourself as the creator. God is the Creator, and when you experience yourself as the creator, you experience yourself as Divine.

Earlier I told you that the entire universe is composed of one thing, acting differently. Your scientists are now calling this one thing the basic energy of life, manifesting as minuscule "superstrings" vibrating at different speeds. The variations in these vibrations produce the variations in the physical matter that makes up all things in the universe.

I also said that *you* were composed of the same thing. Now once you know this, and once you know that "matter" shows up differently depending on the differing vibrations of these superstrings, all you have left to figure out in order to create the physical reality that you desire is *how to make the superstrings vibrate the way you choose.*

It is the speed and pattern of the vibration of the strings that creates particular physical manifestations.

Okay, so what makes their vibration quicken or lessen? What makes their frequency higher or lower?

You do.

I do?

Yes. All of you do. With your thoughts, your words, and your actions.

The things you think, the things you say, and the things you do, send out a "vibe" from the center of your being. Thoughts are nothing more than vibrations. They can be measured, as you know. Words are vibrations of your vocal cords. Actions are your whole physical body vibrating in one way or another.

These vibrations form particular patterns and obtain particular frequencies, and these fluctuations produce particular kinds of disturbances in the energy pattern that is Life Itself. Such disturbances are nothing more than patterned and changing movements of the invisible superstrings, and it is these varying vibrations that produce varying physical matter.

This is the alchemy of life!

Yes. You can alter "life's frequency" by what you are thinking, saying, or doing, thus producing changes in the energy pattern that is "you," and in the energy that "you" emit and send into the world.

The changes in the energy field inside and around you produce new localized fluctuations in the larger Space/Time Continuum within which you exist, and

that is what causes the new physical effects of
your life.

What kinds of thoughts, words, and actions produce the most
beneficial frequencies? I think I know the answer, but tell me
anyway.

Well, of course you know the answer. Positive
thoughts, words, and actions produce the most beneficial frequencies in the superstring vibrations, or energy
patterns, of life.

Meditation or prayer is a high form of energy alter-
ation. Visualizing what you desire is a high form of
energy manipulation. Speaking your word is a high
form of energy adjustment. Such activities alter the
vibration of the superstrings that make up you and
everything around you.

Time itself is also experienced differently depending
upon the vibrational shifts that occur with changes in
the state of your awareness. If you are in an altered
state of consciousness, time can seem to stand still, or
to speed up dramatically.

Many is the person who has been deeply in meditation for what seemed like an eternity—only to find
that barely a few moments have passed in the External
Reality. Conversely, it is not unusual for a person to be
in prayer or in quiet contemplation for what seems
like a short time, then to look up at the clock and discover that an hour or more has elapsed.

People experience this and then say that time can

feel contractible or stretchable. What is actually happening is that you are moving more slowly or more
rapidly through the Corridor of Time, which is not
contracting or stretching at all.

This is an extraordinary short course in metaphysics. Maybe
we should call it metaphysical cosmology. *Metaphorical* metaphysical cosmology at that. But we should not really label this
"science," because we'll have a lot of people debunking it on sci-
entific grounds. And rightly they should, because based on what
science now knows, much of this will make no sense.

You would be surprised at how much of it will make
perfect sense.

Having said that, how much of this short course is necessary,
do you think, in order to understand life and death? I mean,
we've gotten into so many things here . . .

It can be very helpful to know, at a theoretical level,
what is going on in the *process* of life and death, as well
as how, and why.

Okay, then, let's explore further this idea that there are many
"routes" through Space/Time—

—an endless number—

—and that I may take any route that I wish.

You may. Including, as we've already noted, one that
you took before. In fact, you do this quite often.

And when I do, I may experience the same things that I experienced before, or I may not, depending on what I choose, yes?

That is correct.

But how does the process work? How do I make this choice?

By what you look at, by what you give your attention to. What you look at is what you will experience.

Yes, you've told me that. Still, I need just a little more help here. I think I'm beginning to understand this, but I need just a little more help.

Remember when I asked you to imagine markings on the tunnel? Remember the markings on the Corridor of Time?

Yes. You said they were actually pictures.

That's right. You have a very good memory. Well, now in your imagination let's make it a mural. A never-ending mural. It covers both walls of the tunnel, the ceiling, and the floor. The mural is all around you. Can you imagine this?

Yes.

Okay, good. Now let us say that on your first passage through the "time tunnel" your attention is captured at one particular point by a portion of this mural. The mural has many parts and they are all around you, but you have moved to and are looking at one part and that is what you are focused on. Then you keep on moving, but you remember that at that place in the tunnel you experienced one part of the picture. You now call this your "past." Are you following the metaphorical storyline here?

I think so. Go on.

On the next journey you make through this particular tunnel of "time," at the same point you passed before, maybe you move to and look at a different spot in the mural. You see something entirely different. You focus on another part of the picture. You can do this in the same "moment" by moving left to right, up and down, forward and backward, or *circumferentially* in the Corridor of Time.

Remember, there are pictures all around you in every "moment" of "time." If you only move forward and back, up and down, left and right, through the corridor, you limit your options as to which other pictures you can move to and look at. But if you move circumferentially, you can explore all the pictures that exist in one single moment, by moving around the "ring of time" that represents that particular nanosecond. It is like moving around every edge of a snowflake. Remember that I have said, every Moment is like a snowflake. There are no two alike in all of Eternity.

And if I change one single thing in any of those rings, I change all the "pictures" that follow.

Exactly. Thus it is that you can take the same path, but see different things.

Gosh, I really am Lord of the Rings!

> You are, indeed.
>
> The ring, or circle, has always been a sacred symbol signifying eternity, completeness, endless love, and the endless journey.

But if I am on this endless journey, won't I recognize—I mean, the mural is all around me . . . won't I recognize anything at all?

> Oh, yes. When you travel in a spiral through the Corridor of Time, very often your eyes will light upon a portion of the "mural" that you saw before, and you will say, "I have been here before! Everything is exactly as it was then."

Déjà vu!

> Precisely.
>
> Now sometimes when you travel around a "time tunnel," you will experience yourself receiving a "message" or getting "instructions." It could be a warning . . . "Don't move that way. Don't focus on that part of the mural." Or it could be an invitation . . . "Look at *this* part of the mural. See this picture, over here."

Yes! I've had that experience! Who is telling me that? You?

> You. YOU are telling you that. It is the Individuation of the Singularity that is sending you these "instructions" that come in the form of what you call "hints" or "hunches" or "women's intuition" or a "psychic hit."

I'm *talking to myself.*

> You are.

My "future self" is talking to my "present self."

> You could put it that way. And if you listen carefully to your Self, you can experience any point in "time," or your whole trip through the tunnel, in an entirely new way.

So . . . let me see if I've got this right . . . I'm continually moving through Time and Space, and either I'm taking new routes altogether—

> —what you would call "living different lives"—

—or taking the same route as before.

> What you would call "living the same life over again," during which you may experience déjà vu—the sense of having "been there before."

But if all of this is happening at the same *moment* . . .

> It is. Remember, there is only one *Applorange.* The Space/Time Continuum is the Singularity. There is nothing else BUT the Singularity.

. . . then I must exist *within* the Singularity at several different points simultaneously. We touched on this a little before, when we explored the idea of alternate realities. Are you saying that I can be in two places at once?

> You can be in *many* places at once, not just two. And you are.

I'm the Individuation of the Singularity experiencing life sequentially simultaneously!

> And you now understand completely.
> The "you" that is You—the All that is the Individuality—has expressed itself multitudinously.

I always knew I had multiple personalities!

> In metaphysical terms, you are experiencing your Self as the Multitudinous Individuality.

My god, no wonder you have to circle back over this stuff. This all has countless layers. It seems that I am the multitudinous individuation of the singularity, experiencing life sequentially simultaneously.

> You see how hard it is to put all this into words? You have to make up words and phrases that don't exist in order to even get close.

But I know what you are saying! You are saying that I have lived many lives, and that I have lived THIS life many times.

> That is correct. Except you would understand this even better—you would be stating it more accurately—if you did not use the past tense.

I *am living* many lives, and I *am living* THIS life many times.

> Now you have it exactly.
> Almost.

Almost?

There's one more little detail ...

What is it?

You have painted the mural.

What?

And you can alter the painting at any time.

WHAT?

You can add to it, white out any part of it, color over or change the color of any portion of it each time you pass any point in "time." You may alter the painting in any way that you wish, whenever you wish.

Oh, my God, the superstrings are my brushes!

Good work! Great analogy.

So nothing EVER has to be the way it was before!

That is right.

This means that the possibilities are *endless.*

Correct.

Then ... then ... this could go on *forever.*

It does, my wonderful One. It does.

Death is the passageway between the physical world
and the spiritual realm . . . and back again.

So I am "painting the mural" in the Corridor of Time by changing the vibration of the energy of life that swirls in me and around me.

Yes.

With your thoughts.

You are "painting" ahead of you with your thoughts.

And with your words.

Everything you say paints a picture of who you think you are, and how you imagine that life is.

And with your actions.

Everything you do expresses something about you. You are putting the pictures of every possibility into the mural. Everything that you ever thought was possible—every hope, every dream, every worry, every nightmare—is all in the mural.

You have mixed your metaphor with quantum mechanics, which says that all possibilities exist.

> Exactly.

And I experience the possibilities that I look at.

> That's it. That's the metaphor AND quantum mechanics, all rolled into one. Remember, it is quantum physics that says that everything observed is affected by the observer. The metaphor says, "The part of the mural you pay attention to is what you experience."

Physics and metaphysics are saying the same thing. They're just using different language!

> Now you are piecing it together. You are understanding more and more every minute.
> The point here is that you have lots of thoughts, but you don't have to pay attention to all of them. In fact, you couldn't if you wanted to. You would go out of your mind.

Yet there *are* those who see more of the mural at once than most of us. They are often labeled as having "attention deficit disorder."

> In fact, this is not an attention *deficit*, but an attention *surplus*. Such individuals have a wider attention span than most people. They see across a broader spectrum of the Ultimate Reality. They "take in" much more. After you understand this, you begin treating

such children and adults differently, calling many of them "gifted," or "psychic," or "indigo."

Wow, you are explaining *everything* here.

No, not everything. It would take many more conversations across the eternity of time to explain "everything." But it is good that we are having this conversation, limited as it must be. For when you even *begin* to really understand how life works, and what death is all about, then you may at last feel at Home with God.

You have yearned for this experience for so long. It is time now. It is your time to evolve to the next level, to grow in your understanding. That is why your soul brought you here. That is why you are creating this experience. That is why you are producing this dialogue.

I am teaching myself how to make life work here.

Yes. You have been teaching yourself that all along. Now you are simply picking up speed. You are giving yourself the theoretical basis for life, using a bit of metaphor, a bit of science, a bit of metaphysics, and a lot of spirituality.

I got it. I see that. So now what I want to know is what I can do with, how I can work with, the pictures that I, myself, am painting into the *Mural of Possibilities* along the Corridor of Time.

When you see a picture in your mind's eye of something that you do not choose as part of your reality, don't give it a second look. Picture something else.

This holds true for everything in life, doesn't it?

It does. And it also holds true for "death."

Which is the amazing thing. I mean, it's amazing enough to think that we are creating our own reality during life. It's absolutely mind-altering to think that we are creating our own reality after "death."

It's not so amazing when you realize that there IS no death.

Yes. Now I understand the Seventh Remembrance, "Death does not exist," at a much deeper level. What you mean by that is exactly what you said earlier: Death does not exist *as we have pictured it.*

Go on with that.

I hear you better now when you say that there *is* this experience that we call "death," but it is not an "end" to our lives—or really, an end to anything. "Death" is really at the center of everything. It's "the core of the apple."

Yes. It is the central experience of your life. It is what leads you to the Core of Your Being. It is where the seeds of new life are found. The seeds of new life are always at the Core.

"Death" is something you move through in order to get to the "other side." It is the passageway between the physical world and the spiritual realm *and back again.*

I think that this is the greatest revelation of the metaphor. Even when a soul lives within the spiritual realm, there comes a day, there comes a time, when it "dies."

> There comes a time when it is "born again." This is the time when the soul becomes physical once more.

And this happens when it comes through the Core and reemerges back into the physical world.

> Yes.
>
> You are seeing everything perfectly through this metaphor of the *Applorange*.

But that would mean that, to the soul . . .

> That is precisely what it would mean. You have just hit upon . . .

THE THIRTEENTH REMEMBRANCE
Birth and death are the same thing.

The experience of death and the experience of birth are identical?

> At the Center of the Core of Your Being, yes. To your soul, yes. Both are simply energy attenuations, acting not unlike power transformers, facilitating transitions from one world to the next.
>
> The words *death* and *birth* could well be eliminated from all of your languages. The word *creation* could easily be substituted in both cases.
>
> Birth and death are moments of creation. They are the Prime Moments.

So instead of saying that so-and-so was "born" today, we could say that so-and-so was "created" today. And instead of saying that so-and-so "died" today, we could say that so-and-so was "created anew" today.

Yes, that would be wonderful! That would be far more accurate!

Very few people understand "death," and so, many have painted it as the saddest experience. Remember I said that you may paint the mural any way that you wish . . . and the picture you create is the picture you will experience.

But that's *terrible.* It's not my *fault* if I was told of horrible things by people I trusted!

You have let other people paint your pictures for you?

We all have. Most people were told of judgment and damnation by their religions—priests, ministers, rabbis, mullahs, and others whom they deeply trusted to know and tell the truth.

Yes. That is what makes religion, and what religion says to its followers, so critical.

But if there is no "hell" or "judgment" and "damnation" in Ultimate Reality, why should a person have to experience that?

As we have declared repeatedly now, a person does not *have to* experience that. A person would be *choosing to* experience that. You do not have to follow the dictates of any belief system, nor to accept and

embrace the teachings of any person. You may make a
conscious decision to seek your own truth. Indeed, to
create it.

You keep saying that I can *create my own truth.*

You do it every day, by what you believe.

But if, as you told me earlier, a person is constantly creating at
three different levels—the subconscious, the conscious, and the
superconscious—why in the world would the superconscious, the
highest part of us, not choose something other than damnation?
Why wouldn't it create something else?

You have been listening to every word I've said,
haven't you?

We are talking now about life and death in the most detailed
and important way ever. Of course I have.

Good. Because I have listened to every word that
YOU have said.

What's that supposed to mean?

You'll see.

You can't change your experience—in this lifetime
or the next—until you know how you've created it.

Go on. Go ahead with what you were asking me.

Well, this is all becoming very theoretical here, and I really don't know—I've said this before—I really don't know if this has any value . . .

Again let me promise you that looking at all of life in this larger way has enormous value. It helps you to crystallize your thinking about what is going on here, to deepen your understanding. This prepares you for both life *and* "death."

Then if, as you've said, the superconscious is the part of us that holds the larger agenda of the soul, and is constantly leading us to our next most appropriate growth experience, why in the world would it draw to us the experience of judgment, damnation, and hell in the afterlife? Why would it allow our conscious mind to accept and to embrace such an idea?

Do you remember now what you said, in your own words, in the letter to Jackie?

I think so . . .

> In that letter you said, "Sometimes the Soul chooses things at a subconscious or a superconscious level that it would never choose at a conscious level."
> You said that it does this "in order to fulfill its Larger Agenda."

So you're telling me that the Larger Agenda of my soul is to experience judgment, damnation, and hell?

> That may very *well* be the Larger Agenda of your soul. And remember, your experience of hell involves nothing of what you call "suffering."

Still, if there *is* such a thing as a "superconscious," I can't believe that it would deliberately choose to cause me to experience hell, with or without suffering. Besides, you've made a great effort to explain to me that we experience at the moment of our death what we *believe* we are going to experience. You've told me that our Afterlife experience is thus a result of *conscious choice.* Now you're telling me just the opposite! Now you're telling me that it's the result of my *superconscious* choice! *Which is it?*

> Both.

Both?

> Consider the possibility that it may be the choice of your superconscious to create whatever you choose to create *at the Conscious Level.*

Why? Why would it do that?

> Perhaps so that you may come to Completion in Experiencing and Feeling what you Know about yourself.

Which would be—?

> That you are the Creator of your own reality.

The superconscious part of me is going to allow the conscious part of me to experience myself in that way, as a creator, *even if what is being created is bad for me?*

> There is no such thing as "good" and "bad." They do not exist in Ultimate Reality. Good and bad are judgments made in the mind.

Who cares where I am making the judgment? If I am in "hell" and my mind says, "This is hell," that's enough for me. It's not going to matter to me that it's "all in my mind"! All that will matter to me is *what I am experiencing.* It's not going to be very important to me HOW it has come to pass that I am experiencing that.

> Ah, but it should be.

Why?

> Because only when you know "how it has come to pass" can you change it. You can't change your experience—in this lifetime OR the next—until you know how you've created it.
>
> Now if you *know* that the "hell" you are experiencing is being created by you consciously, solely in your

mind, then you will know the formula by which you can end that experience immediately.

Which is?

You have to be out of your mind.

I'm *going to be when I finish this conversation!*

Just stay with it, my friend. You are doing very well.

People who experience heaven instead of hell are *all* told that they are "out of their mind." They are confronted with the same set of circumstances as everyone else, but they experience them in a different way.

Like Don Quixote.

Like Don Quixote. Some people, as we said before, experience life as hellish, while others experience it as heaven on earth.

Yes, well, that does depend on what is going on in their life, doesn't it?

And why do you think that what is "going on" is going on?

Because of how they are thinking.

That is correct. Or, to put it another way, so that you are not likely to forget it:

What is going on
    in people's lives

is what is going on
   in people's lives
because of what is going on
   in people's minds.

What is happening is what we *think* is happening, and what is *going* to happen is what we *think* is going to happen.

To a large extent, that is true.

This is where the three Tools of Creation (thought, word, and deed) and the three Levels of Experience (subconscious, conscious, and superconscious) come in.

Right. And thought is a very powerful tool because it is used at all three levels.

What about words? Aren't words used at the superconscious level? Isn't that how the superconscious communicates with us?

No. Words are creations of the mind. When you move from the conscious mind to superconscious awareness, you will find that there are no words for it.

If you move to this level of awareness in meditation, during sacred dance or ritual, or by some other means, you will find in that place that there are only feelings (or vibrations).

When most people feel something, they will immediately explore that feeling with their conscious mind and try to "put it into words." This may or may not be useful.

The master does not impulsively do this. The master simply feels the feeling, allows the feeling, and experiences the feeling fully. Then the master decides whether there will be any benefit in trying to put that feeling into words.

Feelings are your first thought, your pure thought. A feeling is a wordless thought. It conveys a great deal without "saying" anything. Feelings are the language of the soul.

Words are your second thought. They are your attempt to conceptualize your feelings by translating them into audible utterances. Words are the language of the mind. Masters have a feeling and often don't give it a second thought. This avoids all manner of life complications. It makes the path less arduous.

Actions are your third thought, and are often an afterthought. They are your attempt to physicalize what you have conceptualized. Actions are the language of the body.

By the time you put feelings into words and words into action, you may have lost a lot in the translation. The master knows this, which is why the master is very careful and moves with great deliberation from one level of experience to another—if he moves to another level at all.

Most human beings are focused most of the time on things that do not really matter.

Speaking of the Tools of Creation, you have made a real point here of letting us know that death is a moment of creation.

Because it is, and very few people think of it this way.

If more people did, there might be a lot less sadness surrounding death.

There would be no sadness at all. Not for the person departing. There would be celebration.

Death is a time when people become very powerful, because who they are is magnified through the process of death itself.

And that process is, again?

"Death" is the energy that propels you through the Core of Your Being and into your next reality.

We're going to get back into this business of

"energy alignment" here that we explored before.

"Birth" and "death" are moments of Pure Creation because they align or "fine-tune" the energy that is Life Itself, increasing the vibration of its frequency and manifesting as matter in the physical world, or decreasing the vibration and manifesting as invisible energy in the spiritual realm.

It is in this way that entire universes are born. It is in this way that you were born.

And—now here is the secret—the energy with which you enter birth is "what matters." That is, it is what *changes into matter,* manifesting in the physical world.

The exact opposite occurs at the moment of death. Thus, you create with death by what you bring *into* death from the physical world and you create with birth by what you bring *into* birth from the spiritual realm.

Again, I've never had it explained to me like that. So many things are being made clear here.

Good, because this is critical. What you bring into the experience of your death will be brought in either consciously or unconsciously, either with full awareness or with a complete lack of awareness of what you are doing.

That is why the conversation we are now having is so important.

The purpose of this conversation is to *make you fully aware of what you are doing.* You brought your Self to this conversation so that you could remind your Self of this:

You are creating your reality by the vibration, by the energy, that you send out.

NOW YOU CAN SAY THAT YOU'VE HEARD ALL OF THIS BEFORE—BUT YOU ARE NOT *ACTING LIKE IT.*

THAT IS WHY YOU KEEP TELLING YOUR SELF THIS OVER AND OVER.

What would it "look like" if I *were* "acting like it"?

If I really understood this and didn't need to have this conversation circle back, again and again, over what I "think" I already know, what would that look like?

First, you would never entertain negative thoughts in your mind again.

Second, if a negative thought *did* happen to slip in, you would get it out of your mind immediately. You would think of something else, deliberately. You would simply *change your mind about that.*

Third, you would begin to not only understand Who You Really Are, but to honor and demonstrate that. That is, you would move from what you Know to what you Experience as the measure of your own evolution.

Fourth, you would love yourself fully, just as you are.

Fifth, you would love everyone else fully, just as they are.

Sixth, you would love life fully, just as it is.

Seventh, you would forgive everyone everything.

Eighth, you would never deliberately hurt another human being again—emotionally or physically. Least of all would you ever do this in the name of God.

Ninth, you would never mourn the death of another again, not even for a moment. You might mourn your loss, but not their death.

Tenth, you would never fear or mourn your own death, not even for a moment.

Eleventh, you would be aware that everything is vibration. *Everything.* And so you would pay much more attention to the vibration of everything that you eat, of everything that you wear, of everything that you watch, read, or listen to, and most important, of everything that you think, say, and do.

Twelfth, you would do whatever it takes to adjust the vibration of your own energy and the life energy that you are creating around you if you find that it is not in resonance with the highest knowing you have about Who You Are, and the greatest experience of this that you can possibly imagine.

Excuse me, but how does all that happen? For instance, how can I become "cognizant" of the "vibration" of a piece of clothing, or a meal listed on a menu, to say nothing of something that I'm thinking, saying, or doing?

It's really quite simple. Tune in to how you feel.

Now I can just see someone saying, "Boy, what a piece of new age jargon—*get in touch with your feelings.*"

Those who see it as jargon will experience it as jargon. Those who see it as wisdom will open the door to a whole new world.

Any suggestions on how to do that?

It is just a matter of focus. Most human beings are focused most of the time on things that do not really matter. Yet if they were to take a few moments each day to focus on what does, they could change their whole lives.

Your body is a magnificent instrument of highly sensitive energy receptors. Believe it or not, you can run your hand six inches over the food in a buffet line and, without touching it, feel whether it is of benefit to you to eat that right now. You can do the same thing with clothing that you are picking out of a closet to wear for the day, or that you are thinking of buying in a store.

When you are with another person, if you will stop listening to what you are thinking and begin listening to what you are feeling, the quality of your communication with that person will skyrocket—as will the quality of the relationship itself.

When you are confused and perplexed and looking for answers from the universe, if you will just turn off the part of you that desperately wants to figure things out and turn on the part of you that knows it has access to every answer—if you will stop trying to decide what to *do* and start choosing what you wish to be—you will find dilemmas dissolving and solutions appearing magically right in front of your face.

As for measuring the vibes of thoughts or words, there are very *few* people, actually, who cannot tell you whether they are feeling light or heavy about thinking or saying something. Most people can assess this pretty quickly.

Yes, but—and here is where the screw turns—*very few people ever do.* At least, that's my observation. Gosh knows, I certainly don't nearly enough.

Then you may wish to start.

Because you are right, very few people use their intuitive and psychic abilities to go deep within themselves and get in touch with their feelings before they think or say or do something. Very few people even do it afterward. If you did this you would allow yourself to be satisfied with nothing less than lightness. You would have nothing to do with anything that has heavy vibes. You would seek to lighten the vibration of everything that you observe, create, experience, and express. You would call this "enlightenment," and you would see amazing results in a very short period of time.

The alchemy of the universe is really quite extraordinary. Your dictionaries define "alchemy" as "an inexplicable or mysterious transmuting," and it is just that, being the process by which energy and matter are manipulated to create specific and particular manifestations in both individual and collective reality.

And that brings us to ...

THE FOURTEENTH REMEMBRANCE
You are continually in the act of creation, in life and in death.

I have explained to you many times now how creation occurs. What it would be beneficial for you to understand is that it occurs continuously. That is, *it never stops*. Every thought, word, and deed is creative. Every vibration released from the Core of Your Being recreates you, and your entire reality, anew. And you are being changed in every single moment. Your future is produced in tiny increments, not in one fell swoop or with one major decision. It is the *increments* to which you must pay attention. Then the "major moments" and "monumental decisions" will take care of themselves.

Death and birth are the biggest acts of creation because these are the moments in the Eternal Life Cycle when Essential Energy transmutes itself to produce specific manifestations in the spiritual realm (at death) or in the physical realm (at birth).

This is really getting to be an amazing discussion. First we got into perception theory and quantum physics, then superstring theory and metaphorical metaphysical cosmology, and now we're into alchemy! *Whew.*

But you indicated that before this conversation ended you would be talking to me in much more depth about the moment of merging, or reuniting, with the Essence. Is it okay if I ask about that now?

Of course it is. But I must tell you again that plain words are going to fall short as we try to describe the indescribable. Perhaps it would help if we created another picture *within* the picture now in your mind ...

Again with the pictures.

Yes, well, as you said, a picture is worth a thousand words.

Now we have already established that at the center of the *Applorange* is the Core, yes?

Yes, I get that.

Good. Now see if you can picture this Core as a room or a chamber of some kind. Give it a shape and a color if that helps.

Okay. I've made it a shiny, metallic, golden bronze cylindrical container.

Great. Make it any shape or color that you wish. Now picture a sign on the door leading *into* this chamber. The sign reads "DEATH." And let us imagine that there is a second door leading into this chamber from its far side. This one is marked "BIRTH."

Do you have this pictured?

Yes.

Okay. Now, the inside of the door marked "DEATH"—the side that you would see behind you once you moved through the door—is marked "PHYSICAL WORLD."

That's where I've just come from.

> Exactly. And on the inside of the door across the room is a sign saying "SPIRITUAL REALM."
> Do you have it? Do you have this pictured?

I do, yes.

> Repeat it to me.

You don't believe me?

> Just to make sure.

Okay . . . we are imagining that the chamber at the core of the *Applorange* has two doors, one on each side. The outside of the doors are marked *Death* and *Birth*. The inside of those same doors are marked *Physical World* and *Spiritual Realm*. Both doors lead inward to the same chamber, the same experience—and both doors lead outward to entirely different experiences.

> You have it exactly.
> Thus, you realize when you are in the chamber that you may move to either door and, opening it, will find life in one form or another. There are two ways out of the Core. One door leads to physical life, one door leads to spiritual life.

I've got it. I see it.

> Okay, one final detail and the metaphor will be complete.

I'm with you. Go ahead.

Remember that previously in our analogy you were moving down a long corridor, or tunnel. We called this the Corridor of Time.

Yes.

There was a mural surrounding you along the walls, floor, and ceiling, remember? This mural stretches all along the corridor.

I remember, yes. I'm painting it as I go.

Good. Now you come to the end of the corridor to a door marked "DEATH." Let's pick up the metaphor there.

Okay. What's next? I enter the chamber?

Not directly. The door does not open directly into the chamber, but into a short passage that leads into the chamber. The door remains open behind you as you step into this passage.

You can feel something "happen" to you as you move into this passage. It feels like a real "*passage*," with the word used as a verb, not as a noun. It feels as if you are *making* a passage, not just *in* a passage. You will move through all three stages of death in this passage—and it will feel as if something is *passing away*.

What is passing away is your sense of yourself as a physical body. It feels as if you still ARE someone, but your "sense of self" does not include a sense of having a body.

What is occurring here in and during this passage is that you are being cleansed of all physical limitation, experience, or sensation. This is the first stage of "death," when you realize that you are not your body—but that you are still very much alive.

The door marked DEATH is still open behind you, and you can look back through it onto the physical world. Now you move into death's second stage and will experience awareness or confusion or whatever you expect to experience. During this second stage you can go back and forth through the open door to the physical world. You will not experience yourself there in any physical sense, but you will feel very much as if you are there nonetheless. Others, still living with their body, may also experience you there.

If you believe that nothing exists or occurs after "death," you will pass during death's second stage into "nothingness," and experience nothing at all. I have described this before.

You may remain in the second stage of death as long as it pleases you to.

What would make you wish to remain at the second stage? Wouldn't you want to go on? Do you even know that there is a third stage of death to go to?

Each experience after death stands on its own. Whether you experience the "hell" of your own creation or the "heaven" of your own creation, the "nothingness" of your own creation, or another created reality altogether, those experiences will stand

alone. You will draw from them whatever remembrances there are to draw from them, and then you
will move on.

During this second stage, do we ever return in spirit to those
loved ones who are still living with their bodies?

The soul may indeed choose to return in spirit to
loved ones remaining in physicality. Often the soul visits
loved ones even before it leaves the body.

Yes, Maggie Berry did that. Many others have done it, too. My
father did that. He came to me in a dream in a way that told me
he was leaving. The next morning I received a call that he had
died the night before.

Maggie Berry was the founder and visionary of Core Matters,
a transformational leadership organization in Denver. Her close
friend and partner in Core Matters at the time of her death, Tom
LaRotonda, told me this astonishing story in June 2005, one
year following the death of his dear friend, who he knew was
terminally ill:

On the morning of June 23, 2004 I was in the office
Maggie and I shared. I had canceled all my appointments. I was
sitting at my desk just dazed, not knowing what to do. I wasn't
sad or angry . . . it just felt so surreal.

Maggie was in hospice and I truly wanted to be with her,
but I fully understood and honored her request to not see
visitors. I had my feet up on my desk and my eyes closed and
began to meditate. Suddenly I heard Maggie's voice so clearly
say "Hi, partner"—a term we used with each other all the

time. Suddenly a vision appeared in my mind ... and there was Maggie standing in front of me, smiling.

I was filled with joy at seeing her. She looked completely healthy and radiant, even though I knew she had lost all her hair and her body had been ravished by the cancer. She came over and we embraced and then she took both my hands in hers and she said to me, "Tom, it's time for me to go. I have said good-bye to everyone but you. I wanted to save your good-bye for last."

She then took me by the hand and we walked holding hands as she thanked me for everything I had ever done for her and she told me how much she loved me ... and I did the same for her.

Suddenly she stopped and released my hand, even though I tried to hold on. She said to me, "It's time ... I have to go. I love you, partner!" and she ran off. As I opened my eyes I noticed the time on my laptop computer. It read 11:44 a.m.

I was unsure of what had just happened, so I walked outside to get a breath of fresh air. I had been keeping my cell phone with me, waiting for any news from Butch [Maggie's husband], however I failed to take it with me just then. After about five minutes I returned and noticed I had a message. It was from Butch, and the call was recorded on my phone as being received at 11:45 a.m.

I called Butch and he said that he had a real strong feeling that I needed to be there at the hospice. I told Butch I would come immediately and he said to hurry, that she might not make it much longer.

When I arrived Butch greeted me and took me into the room. Maggie was still alive but incoherent. She lived about another hour before she took her last breath. It was the most

sacred moment of my life. After she died, I told her family that
I would go back to the office and notify people.

I returned to my office, called the people that I needed to
call, then composed and sent out an e-mail to the remainder of
the wonderful community that she had started and that together
we had built. After that was completed I drove down to my
favorite park in Denver, a place called City Park. I went down to
one of the two lakes that are there and just sat … stunned and
at a loss for words … and cried. Maggie had one message that
she sent constantly to people in every situation: Live a life of joy.
Life is meant to be *joyous.* I tried hard to get in touch with that
message now. I calmed down a bit, and after about an hour I
decided to head back to the office to see if I had any messages.

As I was driving back the traffic was extremely congested
and I found myself getting more and more irritated. Already I
was reverting back to fear and anger after just experiencing
one of the most spiritual moments of my life.

As I sat at a traffic light, fuming, I glanced up and there was
one of those giant-sized SUVs directly in front of me. I looked
down and noticed the license plate. It was one of those
personalized plates and the letters jumped out at me … the
plate said: JOYOUS.

I laughed out loud.

Maggie was sending me a message loud and clear. She was
telling me that she was free and happy, and she was reminding
me that there is only one way to live life. She was reminding
me to be joyous.

I now have a replica of that license plate hanging above my
door, reminding me and everyone who sees it what Maggie's life
and her message to us was all about: the joy of an inspired life.

When Tom told me this story I was really taken aback. I had heard of things like this before, but never actually met a person who had such an experience. So these things do happen.

> Oh, yes. They are very real. Sometime before death, and often in the second stage of death, your soul will "visit" loved ones.

> When you are ready, you will move into the third stage of death. Now the door behind you closes, and you can see only the passage before you. This entire passage presents a much shorter distance than the distance you've just traveled through life. It took you years to get through the first corridor, but you now experience yourself racing through this one, flying forward at an incredible speed.

> There is a pinpoint of Light at the end of this passage, with the passage itself appearing to be getting smaller and smaller. The Light is warm and glowing and feels wonderfully safe and inviting.

Are there pictures on the sides of this passage?

> No. This passage into the chamber that is the Core of Your Being is darker, but not in a foreboding way. Rather, in a soft, warm, and glowing way. The glow is coming from the far end of the passage. It is the Light, and it is a tiny speck at first, but as you zoom through the passage it becomes larger and larger in your field of vision until the Light is ...

> ... All There Is.

*In death, all of your individual identities are shed,
ending the separation of you from you, at last.*

The Moment of Mergence is at hand. The power and the wonder of this moment are indescribable. The information and the knowing that comes from it is, at the conscious level, unembraceable. Only at the superconscious level can it be contemplated, much less absorbed.

Just prior to the mergence, the soul hovers before the Light. It basks in the glow of the Essence. All feelings of fear or apprehension or uneasiness of any kind dropped away during the race through the passage. Now the Essence is radiating pure love, and the soul before it experiences what can only be described as an enveloping sense of being . . . *covered.*

Imagine a pancake being covered in warm syrup, or ice cream being covered in warm chocolate. It feels like that. It feels like a flow of sweet heat to the just-arriving soul. It is a gentle warmth, covering the soul entirely.

Together with this heat comes a feeling for which

there is no single word in the world of physical sensation. It is the feeling of being seen, utterly and completely. Nothing can now be hidden, nothing can now be
overlooked or missed, nothing can escape notice.
Everything "good" and everything "bad" that the soul
may have thought of itself is now spread before it, and,
astonishingly, all of it—the "bad" and the "good"—is
slowly being absorbed by the Light . . . ("accepted as its
own," is how it feels) . . . through a kind of energy osmo-
sis that melts even the smallest sense of shame or
pride, leaving the soul with a beautiful emptiness, holding nothing at all within itself, and experiencing nothing
at all of itself, save Openness.

Now, into this Openness where shame and pride
once coexisted, a new feeling is being poured. First it
felt as if the outside of the soul was being covered,
now it feels as if the inside of the soul is being filled.
Again, words cannot be found to adequately define or
accurately describe this feeling—partly because the
feeling is so huge. It might be characterized as a single,
enormous, conglomerate feeling that encompasses a
thousand individual feelings, now slowly filling the soul.
A feeble attempt would call it the feeling of being
warmly embraced, deeply comforted, dearly cherished,
profoundly appreciated, genuinely treasured, softly nur-
tured, profoundly understood, completely forgiven,
wholly absolved, long awaited, happily welcomed,
totally honored, joyously celebrated, absolutely pro-
tected, instantly perfected, and unconditionally loved—
all at once.

Releasing without the slightest hesitation or regret any and all sense of individual selfhood, the soul moves into the Light. There, it is submerged in something so wondrous that it loses all desire to ever know anything else, melting into the breathtaking glory of unending magnificence, unparalleled beauty, and unequaled completeness of being.

Now you are merged with this Light and you feel dissolved. This "melting" completes the change in your identity. You no longer identify your Self in any way or at any level with the separate aspect of being that you called "you" in your physical life.

This characteristic of the Afterlife actually begins to assert itself in the first stage of death, which is what made it possible for you to experience whatever you chose to experience immediately after you died (including your own hell) without pain or suffering. It will be important to you again in just a moment, when you enter the Core of Your Being.

What occurs here, when you are embraced by the Light, is that you merge with your soul. You come to know at last that you are not a body and not a mind, and not even solely spirit, but all three. This is what the entire death process is about.

Remember that I have said, *the death process is about reestablishing your identity.*

The first stage of the death process releases you from your body, and any thoughts that you may still have that identify you with the body and its appearance.

The second stage of the death process releases you

from your mind, and any thoughts you may still have that identify you with the mind and its contents.

The third stage of the death process releases you from your soul, and any thoughts you may still have that identify you with your soul and its individuality.

Here, in the Total Immersion of Self, you come to a place where Knowing and Experiencing are one, and where what you Know and Experience is that you are not your body, you are not your mind, and you are not your soul. You are something much greater. You are the sum total of the energies that produce all three.

In death, all of your individual identities are shed, *ending the separation* OF you FROM you, at last.

You know what? I thought you were going to say that what I was experiencing here was God, having come to greet me.

That is exactly what we are talking about here.

But you just said . . .

You still seem to think in terms of a separation between You and God, and I am saying—again—that there is none.

While you may not believe this now, at the moment of your physical life, in the Moment of Mergence you will have no doubt of it whatsoever.

Gosh, that sounds wonderful! I can't wait!

You don't have to.

The moment you surrender to love and allow it to lead you
to exactly where your soul wants to go,
you will have no difficulty.

This is another of the several things you have repeated here. I am clear that you wish me to understand that the moment of merging into self-realization, the moment of experiencing my Oneness with the All, is not something I have to wait for until my death.

It is not. You may experience this merging and this realization during your physical lifetime. Many people do.

You've already mentioned meditation, deep prayer, certain disciplines (yoga, tai chi, and so on), dance, and ritual as ways in which people move toward greater harmony, peace, and a state of divine resonance, or oneness. Are there any other "tricks" you can share?

Moving into a place of wonder and awe with all of life, and a simple willingness to experience the fullness of that, a desire pure and true, is all that it takes to open oneself to the possibility of such moments of transcendence. Many people experience this melting into the Oneness quite spontaneously, in the middle of some very ordinary activity. Doing dishes. Vacuuming the carpet. Washing the car. Dressing the baby. Handling an assignment at work. Driving down the road. Standing in the shower.

Suddenly, abruptly, without warning or cause, there is a sense of "no separation," an experience of *unity with everything.* It is usually felt for a split second, and then things go back to "normal," but it is an experience that one never forgets.

What should we do if this happens?

Well, whatever you do, don't ignore it. For many people its meaning is often missed or ignored. If you have, or have had, such an experience, you can go back to it in memory and recapture much of the feeling that was experienced there.

You can use it as a starting place, a jumping-off point, for longer experiences.

There are people who are able to move into this experience of Oneness at will, and who remain within it for extended periods. Some remain within it for the rest of their lives. It is simply a matter of focus, or whole presence centering.

"Whole presence centering"?

Well, we are going to encounter the problem with words again. It is very difficult to describe certain experiences using the limitation of words. That is why I have encouraged you to form pictures whenever you can. Even though the pictures in your mind are metaphors, they will often come closer to bringing you the feeling of "knowing" than words can ever do.

By "whole presence centering" I mean those times when you are wholly *present* in the moment that is occurring *right now* in your life; when there is not a single part of your body, mind, or spirit that is "somewhere else." This is very rare for most people—but it can occur, and people with a real willingness can cause it to occur regularly.

You can, with determination, take your mind off of everything else and bring it to this moment right now. Some of you call this the experience of being "centered," or fully "present."

Ram Dass wrote a book about this called *Be Here Now.* And there is the more recent contribution by Eckhart Tolle, *The Power of Now.*

One way to achieve this state of being is to look into your own eyes in a mirror. This is a deceptively simple and incredibly powerful tool.

The trick is to not turn away if this deep looking becomes uncomfortable. If you are able to hold your own gaze for more than a count of ten, you will begin to experience such compassion and love for yourself that you will almost not know what to do with that feeling. It could be very difficult for you to take in this feeling if you are not used to loving yourself—and most people, sadly, are not. Just be with the feeling and embrace it.

Continue looking deeply and more deeply into your own eyes. If you use a hand mirror, you can be sitting when you do this. Now, all at once, after looking deeply into your own eyes for as long as you can, simply and quickly close your eyes—and be with the feeling that follows. Very often you will feel merged with the Essence. This could last only a moment—or for the rest of the day.

If you have a life partner or a friend with whom you feel close, you may also try a variation of this process by looking deeply into the eyes of another. Again, do not turn your eyes away, even if this deep looking begins to become uncomfortable. It will soon pass, melting into a softness and an inner glow as you feel yourself merging with the Self of the other.

What you are seeing when you look deeply into the eyes of yourself or another is the soul. The eyes are the windows of the soul.

You may remember that, earlier, I said that if you look into the eyes of another, or into your own eyes, and expect to see God there, you will. If you do not, you won't. Either way, however, you *will* become fully present. And becoming fully present to the Here and Now is a very effective way to slough off the distractions and excursions of the meandering mind and bring yourself into a much higher experience of the life you are living.

You cannot look into the eyes of any living creature without becoming fully present. That includes your dog, your cat, even a wild animal. Stop in your tracks and lock eyes with an untamed animal—a lion or a tiger or a bear—and see if you do not feel fully present.

When you become fully present this way with another living being, you may very well start to love them. People do fall in love with their pets, and the feeling is very real.

It is especially difficult to look another human in the eye for any period of time at all without beginning to fall in love. That is why people look away from each other so quickly. They don't dare look each other right in the eye for very long. The love that will follow will overwhelm them. Yet it is because they do not know what to do with that love that they are overwhelmed.

The moment you surrender to love and allow it to lead you to exactly where your soul wants to go, you will have no difficulty. All struggle then will cease, and you will know Oneness.

This is what happens at the Moment of Mergence. This is what occurs at the time of Total Immersion with the Essence. It is a very healing way to start a day—or to end one.

Or to end a *life,* it would seem.

I mean, you're saying, aren't you, that some people can experience this merging, this melting into oneness, during their physical life, but that *all people* experience this at the moment of their death? Do I have this right?

You have it very right. No one is excluded, no one is disqualified, no one is left behind.

What about those who don't believe it will happen?

Belief does not create your experience after the second stage of death.

What does?

Desire.

Wow.
Wow, wow, and triple wow.

The three stages of death are designed to move you, gently and as rapidly as you wish to move, through the process of reidentification.

In the second stage of death you still identify with your mind, and so your experience is dictated by what is IN your mind. Your beliefs create your experience.

Once you drop this identity, your experience is created not by what you believe, but by what you desire. This is the beginning of your experience called "heaven."

You may experience these three stages of death that I have now several times described even while you are alive.

Now wait a minute. I know you said that I could experience the Moment of Mergence while I am alive, but I have not heard you say *this*.

We are talking about the same thing. We are talking about the death of the idea of separation. That is what happens at the moment of your physical death, and that can occur at any time.

The three stages of death are simply the Three Steps of Reidentification. These are:

1. Releasing identification with the body.
2. Releasing identification with the mind.
3. Releasing identification with the soul.

But if we are identifying with none of those aspects of ourselves, then what *are* we identifying with?

Nothing.

Nothing? We are identifying with *nothing at all?*

No thing *in particular.*

As soon as you think that you are something, or that you are NOT that, then you begin to imagine yourself as limited. Yet the Essence is in no way limited. In the Moment of Mergence you identify with the All—which means that you identify with nothing in particular. Nothing at all.

The Buddha understood this perfectly, and achieved it. Many masters have achieved it. Most people do not achieve this during their lifetime. All souls achieve this at their death. That is what death is for.

So this is not something that *could* happen, but something that *does* happen, for everyone when they leave their body.

Yes. And in the third stage of death you encounter the wondrous perfection of who you are as seen through the eyes of God.

That sounds so wonderful. Just . . . so wonderful.

And you will not have seen anything yet. This merging into the Essence is not the end of it. In fact, it is just the opposite. It is the beginning.

There is no suffering of any kind in the Afterlife.

You may remain merged with the Essence as long as you wish, but, as we have explained, you will not wish to remain forever, for you would lose the ability to know the ecstasy of the experience.

The tremendous energy shift that you will experience during Total Immersion will propel you back out of the Esssence, renewed and re-created as the identity you remember, and standing in the Core of Your Being.

The chamber, the core of the *Applorange,* if we stay with our metaphor.

Yes.

Imagine now a large room where the portions of the mural that you looked at when you were coming down the Corridor of Time are mounted on the walls. The entire mural is not there, only the parts of the mural, only the sections of the overall painting,

upon which you focused as you moved through the
Corridor.

These images now hang on the walls like an art
exhibit, and you walk through this "art gallery" slowly,
examining the pictures one by one.

As you explore these paintings deeply, you experience everything that is happening in the painting. Not
just what is happening with *you*, but what is happening
with *everyone else in the painting*.

These images represent each of the moments of
your life, and now, examining them, you have for the
first time a *complete picture* of all that is going on in
every moment.

This is often not what you thought was going on,
and it is always more than you imagined.

Well, here we go again. Is it a coincidence that just as we are
having this conversation I would meet a woman at a spiritual
retreat that I was facilitating in Bristol, England, who told me a
story that echoes your "metaphor"?

I could hardly believe what she was telling me, coming on the
heels of what *you* just told me here! It was as if somebody—some
angel or something—was sending me physical, "real world" confirmation of what I was receiving in this rather way-out dialogue
that we're having here.

I was so taken aback by what this woman told me, and by the
coincidence of it all, that I asked her to write it all down and send
it to me. Here's what she wrote. It's a fascinating story of the
near-death experience of one Elizabeth Everitt of the United
Kingdom:

Dear Neale,

I promised you at the weekend in Bristol that I would write to you with my story, so here goes. Are you sitting comfortably?

I was twenty-five years old and for the first time in my hitherto tumultuous life, I felt truly blessed and content. I had met the man of my dreams (after kissing way too many frogs) and I was seven and a half months pregnant with our deeply wanted daughter. I developed a flu-like illness and was admitted to hospital.

I realised quickly that I had chicken pox and was horrified because, as fate would have it, I also worked at that hospital as a midwife and I had watched the last three similar cases end up in intensive care. I knew what treatment was needed and I knew that I needed it NOW.

In spite of being extremely poorly, I tried to take charge of my own care and harassed unwilling colleagues to take me seriously, but in a black comedy of errors they procrastinated, disbelieved, misdiagnosed, neglected and overdosed me, allowing the chicken pox the opportunity to spread viciously and to infect my lungs.

Ever vigilant and observant, my colleagues thought it might be useful to check my oxygen levels after I had turned blue, and there were shocked gasps when the oximeter announced the level at 64%. All hell then broke loose as nobody could understand why I wasn't already dead.

I was hurtled through the hospital to the operating theatre as an anaesthetic colleague whispered gravely in my ear, "Your blood gasses are disastrous. We will have to deliver your baby to save your life. I'm sorry, do you understand what I'm telling

you?" Apparently, I didn't say anything, but I remember clearly
screaming (obviously in my mind), "Of course I bloody know
what you're telling me. I told you that a week ago, you bunch
of incompetent morons!"

At least ten co-workers swooped down on me in a matter
of seconds. They pulled, poked, stabbed and ripped, in frantic
preparation for an emergency caesarean. I had never before
felt such abject terror or such conviction that "this was it." Self-
preservation was so high that I didn't give a toss when they
couldn't find my baby's heartbeat. "What about me! I'm dying.
For God's sake, help me, please!" I screamed over and over—
again apparently in my mind.

The clearly agitated anaesthetist bent down and
compassionately whispered, "For God's sake calm down, you'll
be out in a minute," and then again as I shed tears of utter
desolation, "and you can stop crying, your mucous membranes
are inflamed enough already, without you making it even more
difficult to intubate you!" He administered the anaesthetic and,
assuming that it had already taken effect, announced to
everyone that despite how it seemed, there was no rush
because the surgeon was "still eating a sandwich . . ."

Broken, terrorised, desperate and alone, I was swept into
the anaesthetic believing that I would die and that nobody
gave a damn.

I came round (although apparently I didn't) briefly after the
operation to find myself being "settled" into intensive care.
There were many workers worriedly busying themselves
around me, but it was as if they were all in soft focus—all
except one, who stood clearly to my left side and was dressed
in a slightly outmoded, starched white uniform. She smiled and

spoke to me with a soft, reassuring voice. "Now, now, you're to let these people just get on with it. It's OK. They know what they're doing. You're safe with me. Sleep now."

Relieved that I had made it through the op and reassured by her implacable calm, I allowed myself to go back to "sleep." Almost immediately I felt pulled into a vortex-type sensation. What the heck was this? As I eddied through it I was jabbed with dozens of sudden flashes of experiences. Each flash paused the ride for what seemed like a second and a lifetime at the same time. In one flash I was stabbed, in another I ran over a dog, and in another I was running for my life in a bog-like field with mustard gas burning my lungs, split-second aware of every molecule of my physical body being ripped apart by an explosion.

These flashes were not just presented as images, they were *relived.* I could taste, hear, smell and see everything. I had no conscious recollection of any of this and yet I knew with certainty that every one of these events had at some time, somehow happened to me.

(Hold it. I have to interrupt here. Didn't you tell me, earlier in this conversation, something about this? When I was asking you what happens when a person dies, didn't you say something about this?

      I did. I said that if you die, and if you believe in re-incarnation, you may experience moments from previous lives of which you have no previous conscious memory.

I thought so. So this is, as the British would say, "spot on."

**With one exception. There is no suffering of any
kind in the Afterlife.**

Hmmm . . .

Elizabeth was having some of this experience on "this
side" of death, and some on the other. She was, truly,
between two worlds. Had she been *fully* in the Afterlife
during this first part of her experience, she would have
experienced no pain or fear or suffering of any kind.

Okay, let's get back to Elizabeth's narrative.)

The rollercoaster rode on, and then as snap fast as it
started, it stopped. All sensation left, there was literally
nothing. Blackness. Initially, I was relieved. Thank you, thank
you, thank you, I called out. The fear subsided and I began to
weigh up my surroundings. Black. Nothing. I waited. Nothing. I
whistled, shuffled and hh-hmmed in my mind. Nothing. Panic
began to seep in and I began to question. "Oh, my God. Am I
dead? Is this it? Really, after all that, an eternity of nothing,
except me?"

Increasing panic. Still, nothing. Increasing panic and anger.
"What, no bright light, no guide to ease my transition? Where's
my dad? The very least he can do is show up! Oh, come on.
NO. Help. Please. What the hell did I do? Am I dead? Where is
anyone? Oh, God, no, please. I want to see my baby. What
about my baby? Is she dead? PLEASE. I'm begging, I don't want
to die."

Nothing. Finally, I was quiet and in a state of numb calm.
"What makes you think you're dead?"

My unconscious ears pricked up. I scrambled my unconscious self together. Hang on, I recognised the voice of the nurse by my bedside. "Thank God, where have you been? Where the heck am I? How do I get out?"

"What makes you think that you're dead?"

"Yes, yes. OK. I get it. I'm not dead because I can hear you. What, am I in some weird anaesthetic reaction?"

Dramatic sigh . . . "WHAT MAKES YOU THINK YOU'RE DEAD?"

"Okaaaay. This is weird. Who are you and why do you keeping asking me that?"

"You asked me. Now, what makes . . ."

And so an exhausting discussion began, which seemed to have lasted for days. As I ranted and raved at how unfair, unjust and cruel it was that I was here, wherever the bleep "here" was, she countered my every argument. She challenged my right to live, questioning what made me any more special than anyone else. I was incandescent with rage as I just couldn't get through to this dense maniac.

And then the flicker-book started. You know, just like the book of stick men pictures that you draw in sequential frames and then thumb through to animate it. As it started, I recognised the characters from the movie. This was my life. "Ah, ha!" I sneered, "that old chestnut, I must be dead if my life is flashing before my eyes." No response, just the deep sigh and WHAM!

I was struck deep down to my soul as I felt the full impact of every frame. They flickered past in an instant and yet I swear that I felt the full force of every single moment not just as if I were reliving it but as if every other soul affected by it were also reliving it through me.

These were not the catalogue of moments from my life that I would have compiled given any conscious thought. There were very few momentous, easily recalled events. This was not my airbrushed autobiography. For much of the time the images ran in date order from birth onwards, but there were times when the events were connected in some way and then the images lurched forwards and backwards in time, giving me the full understanding of the consequences of whatever the thought, action or deed may have been.

They were recollections from the full spectrum of emotions, what I would now recognise as moments when I had the opportunity to either show or be shown aspects of divinity. I realised that most often it was not the high-drama times of my life that had the most impact. It was the effect of the seemingly unremarkable events that rippled through time. From the hurt and distress a casual catty comment had made, to the unbridled joy and achievement of riding my bike without stabilisers for the first time.

I remember the emotion and truth of each frame as if it is now imprinted on me, but I struggle to remember with any clarity the specifics of the events attached to it. It is as if the physical events lost their significance once their value was understood. As I recollect it now, I never felt judged and I didn't judge myself—I simply understood that I had seen my true self.

Once the flicker-book finished, I was literally exhausted. I still clung to the idea that I had to win the argument, that I had to prove my right to live, and yet the flicker-book had taken almost all of the wind right out of that sail and a desperate desire to hold my child and be with my loved ones was all that I had left to fight with.

Even that ardent wish was somehow subdued by the aftermath of the life-review. I tried to argue, but my heart wasn't in it. Every statement or question was offset by a perfect response. Finally I whimpered, "You know what. You win. I can't fight anymore. I have nothing left to give. I give up."

Almost before I had even thought the words, I felt immediate relief. The healing that I had bitterly thought was fruitless flooded into my existence and literally enveloped me in a buffer of unconditional support. It was nurturing, reassuring and energizing, and it was as if all those wonderful souls were right there with me, holding my very existence in their arms and keeping it safe.

Suddenly, I was swept from that wonderful place into a phenomenal experience. I have no idea how but I experienced myself flying over a landscape of snowcapped mountains, vast lakes, forest and grassland. I flew over and past a tribe of Native Americans, unlike anything I have ever seen them pictured or described as. I watched a mother watching her children with such serene pride that it was awe-inspiring and then I flew past them up to the top of an imposing mountain in the distance.

Right at the top I came face to face with what I presumed to be a guide, he was a Native American chieftain and as I looked into his well-worn, lined faced and was captured by his eyes, what desperation I had left dissolved. I felt with every fibre of my being that he helped me realise an utterly profound truth but all I can consciously remember is that he told me, "You must be patient, but you will be three."

And in an instant I slept and seemingly instantly woke in Intensive Care, and then the hard part began!

I was told that I had been unconscious for nine days in a semi natural/semi drug-induced coma. A couple of my nurses told me that I had gone into respiratory arrest twice during that time and needed the full support of the ventilator at those times.

Most interesting to me, however, was a period of approximately six hours during which my heart was stuck in an unexpected, dysfunctional rhythm called atrial fibrillation. My heart was beating so fast during that time that it was quite literally flickering, just like my "flicker-book." This "flickering" neither worsened or improved my physical condition, and it would not respond to any medication given to resolve it.

Much to the doctors' surprise the fibrillation suddenly and seemingly inexplicably resolved itself. At this point, one of the doctors suddenly remembered a fact from a previous case that she had dealt with and started a course of treatment that undoubtedly saved my life. I believe that once I "gave up" and the healing flooded in, my body allowed itself to respond and vital information was "given" to the medics. That my mind, body and soul were realigning, just as the chieftain had promised—"You must be patient, but you will be three."

My daughter, Lilie, is very much alive and well, a force of nature no less, and I was watching a TV programme and saw the exact landscape that I had flown over. I investigated where it was filmed and we are going to visit there in August. I have discovered many facts about the area that make me believe that there are people and resources there that will help me to continue the healing process.

The individual moments of your life are what you used to create your experience of Self.

Now isn't that fascinating? How close is Elizabeth's experience to what actually happens after death?

It IS what happened to her, as she moved deeper and deeper into the passage between physical life and the spiritual realm. As I said very early in our conversation, the experience is different for everyone in many respects—and there are some things that occur in every case. The "life review" is one of them.

But that life review sounds as if it could be painful. I mean, some of the moments from my own life might be unpleasant, either because of something that I experienced, or because of what I now notice that I caused someone else to experience.

There is no pain or discomfort at all.

Oh, that's right. I forgot.

Remember that you dropped your sense of personal identity with your mind, and with the thoughts you've held about yourself there, in the second stage of death. In the third stage, you merged with the Oneness.

And in that Moment of Mergence I stepped away from my last sense of personal identity with the individual aspect of being that I have called "me." I stood aside from "me," seeing "me" clearly, but not identifying at an emotional level with the being that I was seeing.

Good. You understand.

Now, as we return to our metaphor, you are in the third stage of death, you've passed through the Moment of Mergence, and as you now experience in fullness the Core of Your Being, you see all that is in the "art gallery," all the experiences of your life, and you can look at them objectively, as if you were flipping through a picture book, or watching a movie or studying a great work of art—which each experience is. You study each moment until you feel that you understand it. Then you move on to the next image, the next moment, the next "painting."

In this way you move through and around the entire gallery; you make sure that you have seen the complete collection. Every moment is important to you, because you realize as you examine the individual moments of your life that those moments are what you used to create your experience of Self— and soon you are going to decide how you wish to re-create your Self anew.

Okay, hold it one minute. I'm confused about one thing. I know this is all a metaphor, and not really "how it is"—

—describing "how it is" without using metaphor would make it virtually impossible for you to comprehend.

I understand. But even knowing this is a metaphor, I have to "pick it apart" a little. There is one thing I am not clear about. I thought I "regained" my identity when I emerged from the Essence, when my "meeting with God" was over. Otherwise, how would I know "who I am"?

You do.

Then how is it that I can go through this "life review"—take a look at all these pictures of moments from my life just lived—and not feel anything? I've done some pretty ugly things, I'm sorry to say. And a few nice things, too. How is it, if I have regained the identity that I shed in the early stages of death, that I don't have any feelings of sadness or happiness or suffering over that?

When your "meeting with God" is over, you regain your awareness of the limited identity that you held in your last lifetime, true, but you do not move back into that identity. Rather, you experience your Self as much larger than that, much more unlimited.

Let me see if I can draw an analogy of my own, just to see if I really understand this.

Go.

I've spent a lot of years in the theater, working in both community and professional theater in six states. So this is how I suddenly find myself thinking about what you're telling me . . .

It would be as if I had stepped offstage after playing a role in which I had very limited abilities or skills, then took off my costume, changed into my street clothes, and stepped out of the theater and into the world as a fully capable and powerful being.

On the outside of the theater there's a marquee display with flashing travel lights and photos of me in many of the key scenes from the show. I see myself in these pictures, in which I am grimacing or smiling or crying or shouting with terrible anger, but of course, I have no internal or emotional reaction to any of this. I know it is not me—that I am standing there looking at these photos—but when I was inside, on the stage, the suffering and the pain and the joy that I displayed not only felt very real to the audience . . . *it even felt real to me.* That's how good an actor I am!

Still, looking at the photos now, I see how I might have played some of the scenes even better—or changed some scenes altogether. And so I determine to do that at the next performance. Then I'm on my way. First stop: the library. I want to know more about this character that I'm playing!

> Bravo! That's a very good analogy! That is very close to what you experience as you move through the Core of Your Being reviewing the "art gallery" of moments from your life. And as you leave the Core of Your Being you DO in a sense "go to the library to find out more about your character."

But please tell me again, why do I bother? Why ever leave the Core? Part of me keeps wondering, even after all this explanation—

why do I, why *would* I, ever leave the Essence? Why wouldn't I remain immersed forever? Wouldn't that be "heaven"?

It is the nature of Life to express itself. That is what Life does. It cannot *not* do this, or it would not be. Now change the word "life" in the above sentence. Notice that "life" can also be called "God," "That Which Is," "the Essence," "the Energy," or whatever else you wish to call it. No matter what word you use, you are still talking about Life.

In the process of self expression, Life quite *literally* "expresses" Itself. That is, It *pushes Itself out* FROM Itself, giving birth to Itself as an aspect OF Itself, that it might Know Itself in Its Own Experience.

That is a handful, there. That is a lot to digest.

Take it slowly. Take it easily. Consider it thought by thought, concept by concept:

1. In the process of Self expression, Life quite *literally* "expresses" Itself.
2. To "express" means to "push out." Life *pushes Itself out* from Itself.
3. In a sense, it gives birth TO Itself as an aspect OF Itself.
4. It does this so that it might Know Itself in Its Own Experience.

That is what it really means to be born again.

That is exactly what it means.

And I am "born again" and move away from the Core so that I—in your words, now—may "better come to Know" what I encountered at the Core "as real," through the perspective of distance.

> Well, you've captured it perfectly. This is what the process of death—and birth—is all about. You are constantly moving to and from the Core of Your Being, that you might Know and Experience the true nature of Who You Are. You use distance to Know and to Experience the Totality as discrete or singular expressions of Itself. For when the Totality IS the Totality, it experiences only the Totality, and none of its constituent parts.

What if I can't be any better than I just was? What if I have experienced total mastery in the life I have just lived? Then what? Will the cycle end?

> No. You will simply redefine "mastery."

I'll raise the bar.

> Yes.

So that the game can go on. So that the process can continue.

> Yes. It is the desire and the nature of Life to produce more Life, and to produce it more abundantly.
> Everything grows, and there is no such thing as the end of evolution.
> Remember that always, for that is . . .

THE FIFTEENTH REMEMBRANCE
There is no such thing as the end of evolution.

I have already described to you the cycle of ever-lasting life. Because you seek to re-create yourself anew, as does all of Life, you will move into the spiritual realm, in which you will come to know and understand more of Who You Are and who you choose to be, then you will return to the Core of Your Being and back out into the physical world, traveling the same Corridor of Time in a different way, or a different Corridor altogether, so that you may Know in Your Experience what it is like to be who you have chosen to be.

But how will I come to know who I want to be? I don't understand about that. When do I choose that?

You will choose that when you respond to the Holy Inquiry.

Ah, *finally.*

Nearly every person who is dying
is not dying for the first time.

32

I've been waiting and waiting. So tell me, before I run out of patience. What is the Holy Inquiry?

At the end of your life, in what we have described as stage three of death, you will be asked an extraordinary question. This will be the most important question you will ever be asked, and your reply will be the most important statement you have ever made and the biggest Moment of Free Choice you could ever imagine.

It is so important that all of the angels in heaven will stop to listen to what you are saying. It is so important that all your loved ones will be gathered around to hear. It is so important that God Himself will be present when the question is asked. Indeed, She will be the one doing the asking.

What is the question?

"Do you want to stay?"

I'm sorry? I am going to be asked if I want to "stay"? Stay where? You mean, *stay dead?*

Yes. In human terms, in your languaging, yes. That will be the question.

Do you mean I will have a choice about that?

You have a choice about everything.

That is the point I have been making since the beginning of our conversation. We are now at the end of a ten-year dialogue, and you are still asking the question.

Well, I know I have a choice about everything in my life, I just didn't know I had a choice about my death. Are you telling me that if I don't want to stay dead, I don't have to?

That's exactly what I'm telling you.

That . . . that's not possible. That's not . . . that runs counter to everything I've ever heard. I don't understand. We're given a choice at the time of our death to "go on or go back"?

That is right. That is exactly the choice you are given. And so here is . . .

THE SIXTEENTH REMEMBRANCE
Death is reversible.

I feel like I am on a roller-coaster ride here. It's all I can do to just hang on. What are you trying to tell me here?

Everyone who "dies" is able to make a decision as to how they wish to go on living—and where.

What an interesting way to put it.

It's the *only* way to put it, because that's exactly how it is. Remember, the Seventh Remembrance is that "Death does not exist."

It does not.

When a person does the thing that you call "die," that person is always given a choice: Do you want to experience that the life you have just left is continuing? Or do you wish to experience a reality in which you are moving on, heading toward the spiritual realm?

You mean that everyone who dies has a chance to "come back to life"?

Yes. The soul can, in its experience, "undo" the "death" through which it has just passed.

How? How in the world does it do *that?*

It simply tells God by saying/thinking/feeling: "I don't want to die now. I want to go back."

Each soul is asked the question, "Are you ready? Do you wish to go on?" This is the gentlest question. It is asked of all souls who "cross over" from the physical world.

If the thought/feeling/reply is "yes," the soul continues on its journey to the spiritual realm. If the soul asks to "go back," the soul is "sent back" to the phys-

ical world instantly . . . *arriving a nanosecond before it
"died."*

This *is* a mind-blower. This is even a little upsetting. If this is
true, why would anyone who really loved his or her family not
want to go back? I mean, as wonderful as I'm sure "heaven" is—
and you still haven't described that to me, you still haven't told
me what happens on "the other side"—it will always be there,
waiting for us. Isn't it kind of selfish to stay there when you know
that you can go back, and that your loved ones are hurting so bad
because you are gone?

I don't know if I can believe this. This leaves me feeling . . . I
don't know . . . empty.

Would you rather we didn't pursue this?

Well, you *said it* now. There's an elephant in the middle of the
living room. You expect me to be able to ignore it?

It wasn't meant to upset you.

I'm sure it wasn't, but . . . so tell me, what is this all about?

**It is simply as I have said: after dying, every soul is
given the opportunity to remain in the Afterlife or to
return to the physical life from which it has just
come.**

Yes, I understood that. But please give me the details. When
does this occur?

**It occurs after you melt into the Light. After the
Moment of Mergence.**

Well, that's not very fair. Who on earth can compete with *that?* Why would anyone want to return to physical life after merging with the One? I mean, really.

> Actually, many, many souls do.

What? Why? Are you telling me that many souls would rather return to earth than remain in heaven? That doesn't say much about heaven.

> It says that heaven is exactly what you imagine it to be—a place where you can have anything you wish.
>
> After merging with the Essence, the soul understands many things. It understands that there is no such thing as judgment and condemnation. It understands that nothing negative can possibly occur in the Afterlife. It understands Who and What the soul is. It understands the purpose of Life and the Process of Life. It understands fully and completely the nature of Ultimate Reality. And it understands that the Afterlife will always be there, waiting, waiting, through all eternity.

Or as someone put it in the title of a movie once, *heaven can wait.*

> Exactly. After merging with the Essence, the soul understands, essentially, all that I have been telling you here. But now it understands these things experientially, not intellectually. And then many souls *do* choose to return to physical life. In fact, *most souls do,* at least once.

Most souls do?

> Nearly every person who is dying is not dying for
> the first time. If they choose, this time, to "stay dead," it
> is because they feel really complete with what they
> came here to do. Therefore, do not begrudge them
> their moving on, nor feel angry because they have not
> come back. They came back to you many times to keep
> you company before. Many times.

I'm lost here. I am lost. This conversation has taken me to
many places, and I've breathlessly tried to keep up. I've done, I
think, a pretty good job—but this one is getting away from me.
This one is so far over my head that I don't think I can even
reach for it.

> Try.

I don't know where to begin.

> Ask me a question.

Okay. What do you mean, my loved ones have come back to
me many times?

> I mean just that. I mean your loved ones died and
> then came back to you more than once, out of their
> sense of wishing to be complete with you, and with all
> the rest of what they chose to accomplish in their life.

My mom died, and she was gone. She never came back.
My dad died and that was that.
My brother slumped over the wheel of his car *while he was driv-
ing*, for heaven sake, and my sister-in-law had to reach over and

steer the car to the side of the road and find a way to get her foot on the brake pedal to stop it. And she with the after-effects of a stroke, and half her body not working right!

Now I hate to get *mundane* about this, but if a soul can come back after the moment of its death, if it has that choice, then the least my brother could have done was to get back into his body long enough to maneuver the car over to the side of the road, before someone *else* died.

You have a lot of heat on this, don't you?

I guess so. You're standing there telling me that everyone who has died can come back to life if they want to? You're telling me that my mom and my dad and my oldest brother, who I adored, went to "the other side," were given a chance to come back to us, and all of them *declined?* And I'm not supposed to have any "heat" on that? I mean, talk about your abandonment issues . . .

That's got to be the abandonment issue of all time. The Mother of All Abandonment Issues.

I see. So it's about you, not them.

What?

Someone you love dies, and your concern is about you, not them.

Oh, come on, that's not fair. You just told me something very unorthodox about all this. You just told me that the people closest to me had a chance to come back to their grieving loved ones, and they all said no.

>   But I also said that they all said yes more than once.
>   When they go and they *stay*, it's because they are really
>   "done" this time, really complete. Their final departure
>   was just that. It was their Last Leave-Taking. All the
>   other times, they returned.

All what other times? I don't recall anyone "returning." None
of the people I'm talking about had operating room resuscita-
tions or sudden remissions of illness, or anything like that. When
they "went," they went. Boom. Gone. End of story.

>   Your mom "went" four times.

What?

>   What *you* call your mother's death is what *she* calls
>   her *last* death. You're not counting the several she had
>   before that.

My mother had several deaths *before that?* And *came back?*

>   Let me ask you a question. Do you know if your
>   mother ever had any "near misses"?

"Near misses"?

>   Instances in which she almost died, but missed by an
>   instant.

Oh, you mean where she came within an "inch of death"?

>   Exactly, yes. Do you know if she ever had any expe-
>   riences such as that?

No, I don't. If she did, she never told me about them. Why?

I'm going to tell you now that she had four of them. Of those four, two were after you were born.

Are you kidding me? Is this real?

It is very real. And you should know that those were not instances in which she "almost" died. Those were instances in which she *died* . . . and in all of those instances, she then chose to come back.

This is beyond belief. What are you telling me? Why would she come back?

She wasn't finished. She didn't feel complete. Did you know that she almost died at the time of your birth?

No. No one ever told me that!

It's true. In your present reality, she almost died as a result of bringing you into this world. In another reality, she did. Then she decided to come back. She decided that she wanted to raise you, not leave you to the mercies of the world. So she came back. In your reality it was said that she "almost died."

There were other times, as well, when she died, went to the Afterlife, remembered what she needed to remember, and chose to come back.

Then, when even the youngest of her offspring (that's you) reached adulthood, well on the way to creating his own life, she died "for good." Even then she was young—just a year or so older than you are now. But she was truly finished, complete. She had no more reason to go back. It was time to rest, and to enjoy her next experience—which was, in a sentence, the opportunity to move to the next level in her own evolution. She has done that now. She is now what you would call an angel. She is helping others, as she always did.

I'm not even a little surprised. What about my dad? Where is he?

I don't think it is wise or even beneficial to get into the journey and status of every one of the souls who have populated your life. The soul and the essence of that which you have called your father found total happiness and complete peace following death, of that much you can be sure.

All souls do. Not a single soul does not.

Just a second. Something you said about my mom just hit my ear a second time. Will she never return again to physical form? I thought you said that the process of moving from the spiritual realm to the physical world and back again was eternal and everlasting.

I did. And it is. I did not say that your mother has not returned to physicality. I said that she is an angel.

Angels are *physical*?

Angels are anything they want to be. If they want to be physical, they can be physical. If they want to be pure spirit, they can be pure spirit. Angels travel between two worlds.

> There are angels all around you. Some of them in
> physical form, some of them in spiritual form.

Could one of them be my mom?

> What do you think?

I think so. I've often felt her near me. I thought I was imagining it. I thought it wasn't real.

> Think again.

And my dad?

> He helped you write this book. Do you think it's
> sheer coincidence that you came to this awareness *on*
> *his birthday?*

Oh, my God, this *is* his birthday! I've been thinking of him all
day, and I'm writing this on June 29—his birthday . . . is such a
coincidence possible?

> Your dad says, "Nothing to it."

Okay, okay, enough. I mean, I'm getting spooked here,
because *that is exactly what he would say.* So how about if we move on
here. Tell me, how do you get to be an angel? How do you get
promoted?

> You don't get "promoted." It is not about advance-
> ment through some ranking. It's not about some souls
> being somehow "better" than others.

Well, they could be farther along on the path . . .

> Who is "farther along" on a circle?

But I thought you said . . .

> Listen to me. You are moving through an endless cycle. There is no beginning and no end. You are no "better" and no "worse" than any other soul on the cycle. The whole cycle is holy, and you simply are where you are.
>
> One of the difficulties that humans have created on the earth is that so many hold this idea of "better." It is "better" to be a Muslim, or it is "better" to be a Mormon, or it is "better" to be a Jew or a Baha'i, or a Christian, or it is "better" to be a man, or a woman, or a conservative or a liberal, or a Frenchman or an Italian or a black or an Asian or a Caucasian or a member of the Crips or a member of the Bloods, or whatEVER.
>
> You've got it lined out that one of you is better than another of you, and it simply is not so.

But I have a fair question, then. If it's not about being "promoted," if it's not about "advancement," then how *do* you get to be an angel?

> You choose to be an angel.

You choose to be?

> You choose *everything*. There is nothing that you do not choose.

Can angels choose not to be angels anymore?

> Of course they can, and angels have. You can be an angel for a while, and then not be an angel. Then you

can decide to be an angel again. You can go around in cycles, you can go around in loops, you can travel in spirals, you can move in straight lines, you can "stay in heaven" for eons, you can come right back to earth in the next second—you can have it any way you wish.

Do you have any idea Who You Are?

You're trying to tell me here, and I see that I'm resisting it.

Thou art God.

I am you, simply causing you to remember me.

33

Robert Heinlein put that in a book forty-five years ago.

Another of my messengers.

So I, too, have "come back to life"?

Well, let me ask you this. Have you had occasions when it looked as if you had "bought the farm"?

Sure have. I think I know the kind of thing you're talking about now, and I know I've had instances like that.

Of course you have. Would you like me to describe them to you?

No, no, I know which ones you're talking about . . .

There's one you may not know of. There's one you may not remember. It was in the moments after your

birth. You were premature. You weighed just over four pounds. It was not expected that you would live.

But I did.

> The second time, yes.

I beg your pardon?

> The second time, you lived. The first time, you did not.

Oh, boy. We're off the map here again, folks. We're off the map.

> After you died the first time, you indicated that you did not feel complete with what you moved into physicality to experience.

And what was that?

> Giving to others. You wanted to experience giving to others. You wanted to experience loving. You did your best, by dying, but in the end you felt it was not enough. You wanted to experience more.

Wait a minute. I "died" at birth to give to others?

> You completely served your mother's agenda, and your father's. In that moment, you gave the only thing you had to give, life itself, to completely serve your parents' agendas.

What were their agendas?

They will reveal that to you themselves when the time comes. And it will come.

I can tell you about your own agenda, however, at any time. Your agenda in this lifetime is to experience how to love. Selflessly. Completely. You did that in the first moment of your life. You *gave* your life for another. But, as I said, your experience of giving did not feel complete to you. You wanted to give more. You wanted to keep on giving. So you jumped realities.

I'm sorry?

Remember when we talked earlier about the possibility of alternate realities? When you "die" and then "go back," what you do in actuality is simply move your conscious awareness to an alternate reality. In that reality you experience the moment of your "death" over again, but this time you don't die, you live. In some cases what that looks like is a "near miss." In other cases it might be a surprising recovery, or sudden remission. It is like being inserted in the Time Line in the moments or weeks before you "die," and then throwing a switch that diverts the train, sending it off onto another track.

This is what you did the other times, too. The times you know about, the times you recall. In each of those moments—you remember them?—you thought you were a goner.

I did, for sure.

And you were right. You *were* a goner. I mean, you *left*. You were gone.

I was dead?

Every time.

This is really bending my mind. *I've been dead?*

Dead as a doornail.

And yet here I am, right here right now.

What, you think cats are the only ones who have nine lives?

Yes, you were what you *call* "dead" all of those other times. You went through all the stages. By that point in your life you'd heard about "hell," so you went ahead and created you own "hell" and went through that experience. Then you came to a place of remembering. You remembered that "hell" does not exist. Then you created something else, something much more pleasant, but you were not satisfied. Then you met me, in the moment of Total Immersion. Then you had your Life Review. And then I made the Holy Inquiry and you decided to go back.

You didn't feel "complete," you said.

Now I understand a *lot* better a note someone sent me a few months ago. Wow, now this truly makes sense. Completely.
Read this . . .

Dear Neale,

For whatever it may be worth, I would like to tell you a
little story about what happened to me just before Christmas.

I had been on a work assignment and was reluctantly
separated from my husband for six weeks prior to Christmas. I
had a week in the middle of this assignment to drive the five
hours from Grand Junction to Loveland, CO, and be home for
Christmas. On December 22, at 11 p.m., I began my trip,
hoping to avoid upcoming bad weather the following day. It
was a starry night up until I got through the Eisenhower
Tunnel at Loveland Pass.

I exited the tunnel and found myself in a blizzard of snow
and later a real whiteout. It was pretty hairy driving, and I
asked God to keep me safe. When I hit Denver, the driving got
better. Heading north on I-25 the road became quite dry with
just some snow flurries. I was traveling about 50 mph on a
straight stretch of road when suddenly I hit an ice patch and
my car spun out sideways. It was 4 o'clock in the morning.

I hit the left guard rail straight on and felt sudden intense
pain in the lower portion of my face. I didn't know how badly I
was hurt and got pretty panicked when in the distance, I could
see the headlights of an oncoming truck. My car engine had
cut out and I was stopped in the middle of the interstate. I
knew I would be hit before the driver could see me and stop
on that icy road. I was not thinking clearly enough to get out
of the car and all I could think to do was to try to turn on my
flashers. I was groping about but could not find the button to
turn them on.

Then, a miracle happened. My car started to slide backward

for no reason. It slid onto the right shoulder and touched the right side guard rail—where it stopped just as the truck whizzed by.

The rest of the story is not relevant here. Very briefly told, I was able to start the car and drive another 15 miles to my home. I saw my dentist later that day and he found no fractures, and my loosened teeth will probably tighten up in a couple more months. There was no great damage to me and I consider myself truly blessed to have had this experience.

Some people think I was unfortunate. Some think I was just plain lucky. But I know better, and a few others know too.

With love, Inga Kraus

So "near misses" are really "reruns" with a new outcome. What an idea. A *second chance.* A chance to finish up, to come to completion, to do what we came here to do.

Yes.

And I've been "dead" three times before?

Four times. Don't forget your birthing death.

And even when I was an adult, I came back? After all that living?

You said you had a lot you wanted to do, a lot you still wanted to experience. You said you wanted to do better by your children. You said you wanted to experience loving the women who loved you, instead of

mistreating them. Most of all, you said, you wanted to change the world's idea about God and about life.

What does that last part have to do about remembering how to love?

You said you realized that once the world remembers who and what God is, and how life really functions, it would be nothing for people to remember how to love, and that everybody would love everybody, without condition.

After you remembered what was on "the other side," after you spent some time in the Afterlife, after you realized that "hell" was a figment of your imagination (and that *everything* was), and, mostly, after you met Me, you said you wanted to help the world understand some things. But first, you said, *you* needed to understand some things—experientially.

Like what?

You became homeless at forty-nine, in the middle of your life. You created more life partners—and left them, just as you did the earlier ones. Through these devices you learned more about betrayal, about your own ability to betray others, about how it feels when others betray you. You learned a little about love. You learned a lot about abandonment. Abandonment by Life Itself. You were out there, on the streets, living outside, a tent for a home, for almost a year.

You learned what it was like being broke. So broke

that a dollar looked like a lot of money to you, and two dollars was a fortune. One day you gave away money you didn't think you could afford to give away. Your heart went out to somebody and you just gave them the little change you had. On that day you learned about true generosity. You also learned that there was "more where that came from"—and this was a big remembering. You discovered again the universe's endless supply. Very soon you were rich. Rich beyond your wildest dreams.

And you began changing the world's mind about God. And about life. And about each other. Now you have a better relationship with your children. Now you're even learning—the hard way, still hurting others, but at least learning—the beginnings of a new way to love. Now you write books, and sell millions of them. Now you travel the world, talking to thousands of people. Now you're on radio and television, and even in the movies.

You think this has all happened by chance?

You think this has all happened by chance?

I . . . I . . .

I tell you, *you chose all of this.*

And, of course, you've learned nothing. The term "learned" is just a figure of speech. I use it because you use it. I talk like you do. I use the vernacular that you use. We both know that you have "learned" nothing. You have merely remembered. You *remembered* about abandonment, you *remembered* about generos-

ity, you're trying hard to *remember* about love. You
have brought back to your conscious mind as much as
you can remember about *that which you have always
known* regarding God, regarding Life, and regarding
others.

Where do you think all of this is coming from?

Where do I think all of what is coming from?

All that you're writing right here.

I guess I thought it was coming from you. I thought it was
coming from God.

It IS coming from me. It IS coming from God. But do
you think I am something separate from you, telling
you something new?

Listen to me. I am *you,* simply *causing you to remember me.* Your conversations with God have created a
space, opened a door, allowing you to remember what
you have always known.

Now the final question is not whether you will continue to remember, but whether you will continue to
act as if you do not.

Ouch.

Well, that IS the question, isn't it?

To truly understand Ultimate Reality
you have to be out of your mind.

34

I can't believe what we're talking about here. And I can't believe how public this is. Do I have to put this all in the book?

> You said—I did not say, YOU said—that you were pledged to making this a full and complete and accurate transcript of our conversation, with nothing left out. I was the one who said that you might be tempted to edit it. You were the one who said, no way, it's not going to happen. So now you're remembering something else. Now you're remembering about keeping your word. Doing what you say. Being counted on. Is this Who You Are? It's your choice.
>
> It's always your choice.

Whew. You make it tough.

> Look, you can stop right here. End the book. It's been an interesting book. Don't go any further. You've

said enough. Probably more than enough. For some,
maybe even too much. Just close the computer down
and let it go.

No. We're right at Breakthrough here. This is Breakthrough,
and not just for me. This is Breakthrough for everyone reading
this. Even for those who don't know that it's Breakthrough, it is. I
can sense it.

So where do you want to go?

I want to explore that last exchange a little more deeply. Then
I think we can bring our conversation to a conclusion.

I have one more thing to tell you. One more major
revelation. *Then* we can conclude.

A deal. So let me see if I understand our last exchange. You're
saying that every soul, after the moment of death, is given an
opportunity to reverse the process of death itself. I've got that.
It's a stunning thought, and I get it. It's something you would do.
It makes perfect sense, given how much you love us.

I'm glad that you can see that. Trusting in the love of
God will serve you all the days of your life, and on the
day of your death as well. I do love you. I love you all,
dearly.

So just tell me, how does this all happen? And if we really do
"come back," how does that occur? Not everyone dies in such a
convenient way that they can just be "brought back to life" easily.
I mean, some people die on the battlefield, or in accidents, and
they're lying in pieces. Excuse me for being so graphic, but they

are. Not everyone dies comfortably in bed, so they can just "wake up" and the doctor can say, "It's a miracle!"

> Let's go back just a tiny bit.
>
> After you "die," you move through the first two stages of death, just as I have described. You realize, first, that you are not your body. Then you experience whatever you next expect to experience, based on what you believe. You may have that experience as long as you wish, as long as it pleases you. Then you move into the third stage of death. This is the final stage, when you experience Total Immersion with the Essence, emerge from that experience to move through a review of the physical life you have just concluded, and then decide whether to "go on or go back," as you put it.

I make this decision based on what I've seen in my Life Review.

> Essentially, yes. Based on what you've seen and whether there is anything that you still wish to Know and to Experience as a soul carrying the particular identity that you thought of as "you." In other words, based on whether you feel "complete" or not.

But I thought . . . you know, I really *have* been listening to you very closely here, and I thought that you said earlier that no one dies ever feeling incomplete. You said, very directly, that *no one dies having failed to experience all that they came to the physical world to experience.* There is no such thing as being "incomplete." And you said this is what is meant by . . . *the Eleventh Remembrance:* The timing and the circumstances of death are always perfect.

Everything that was said is what is so.

Yet now you are saying that after a person dies they may feel "incomplete" with something or another, and so may "return to life," so to speak, and relive the moment of their death in a new way that ... that ...

That ... what?

That eliminates the fact that they died.

Exactly. Which means that they *didn't* die. Which means that "the timing and the circumstances of death are always perfect." Which means that *no one dies having failed to experience all that they came to the physical world to experience.*

Yes, but they *did* die and found that they *were* incomplete, and so they went back. But this proves that they *can* die being incomplete.

I see how you would think that, so I will give you now one more piece of information.

The process of what you call "death" is not complete until the soul "passes over" to "the other side."

It is on "the other side" of the *Applorange*, it is in the spiritual realm, that the soul does the joyful work of establishing its identity, and re-creating it anew.

And so, no one "dies" to the old until they "cross over" this threshold. To put this another way, *your death is not final until you say it is final.*

If you indicate, at the moment of the Holy Inquiry, that you do not feel complete, and wish to return to the physical life from which you have just emerged, you may do so, and you will do so instantly.

Yes, but you do this, you said, by "jumping realities." You said the soul jumped to an alternate reality. In that case, the soul in *this* reality *did* die incomplete.

> You're going to think this to death, do you know that?

Interesting turn of phrase.

> Be careful not to think too much. Remember, to truly understand Ultimate Reality you have to be out of your mind.
> But let's not dance away from your inquiry.

No, let's not.

> You asked me once if the soul could be in two places at once.

Yes, I did. And you said it could be in a great many more than two places at once.

> Good. You've remembered that. So now, follow me here.
> If the soul feels incomplete and jumps to an alternate reality in which it does not die, then that soul does not die feeling incomplete. Agreed?

Agreed. But the soul remaining in the *other* reality—

> —wait a minute, I'm getting there.
> The soul "staying behind," so to speak, in the first

reality is *not oblivious to what has happened*. It *knows* that a part of Itself has been allowed to jump into an alternate reality and complete what it wishes to complete. It also knows that *there is no such thing as Time.* So it knows that the other part of Itself has *already completed* what it "went back" to complete. So the soul in the Only Moment There Is, the Moment of Now, moves into the spiritual realm feeling utterly complete.

Whoa. You can talk your way out of anything.

You could say that. But I want to suggest to you that not much is being served by this splitting of metaphysical hairs. I think you might derive more benefit from focusing on the larger principles and the main messages of this dialogue.

Many people on earth get caught up in the minutiae. They want to have everything explained, down to the last detail. You can turn embroidery over and look at the cross-weaving of threads that produces it, meticulously tracing each colored yarn until you have figured all the ins and outs, but you will never enjoy the picture they create.

Look at things another way. Change your "I've got to have all the answers" perspective. Give yourself a chance to see the whole picture. You'll love it.

You do not have to be "ordained" to be a minister in the world. God has ordained you by virtue of your being alive.

Okay, so I "get" that every soul is "complete" when it finally arrives on "the other side." So this is the final piece of the puzzle for me. What happens when we get there? What is this work that we do? And how do we do it?

When the soul says it is complete, when it answers the Holy Inquiry and says, "Let's go on," it moves immediately into the spiritual realm, where it begins acquiring the Knowing of itself as what it experienced when it was merged with the Light.

That is, it begins to have the awareness of itself as a Divine Being. This becomes clear very fast, because in the spiritual realm everything the soul desires, it produces immediately. There is no "time lapse" between conceptualizing something and Knowing it as the Self. This happens because in the spiritual realm the soul creates at all three Levels of Creation simultaneously. In the physical world it rarely does.

So when I "die" I suddenly begin to create at the subconscious, conscious, and superconscious levels all at once?

You do so when you enter the spiritual realm. That is, in keeping with the metaphor, when you get through the Core of the *Applorange* and move on to "the other side."

All the levels of consciousness become One upon the Merging with the light, and it is this single consciousness with which you leave the "chamber"—the Core of Your Being—and enter the spiritual realm.

Likewise, all aspects of being—body, mind, and spirit—have become One.

As well, all three tools of creation—thought, word, and deed—have become One.

And finally, all three experiences of what you have come to call "time"—past, present, and future—have become One.

Everything integrates.

Indeed, "death" is a reintegration. Far from DISintegration, "death" is REintegration. Every triune reality becomes singular. What some have described as the Holy Trinity becomes One.

Because you are now creating with *all the tools of creation at every level of awareness at once*, your creations are *instantaneous*.

I create at the supraconscious level in the spirit world!

Yes, and everything you desire is instantly made manifest in your knowing.

Masters create from this level in the physical world as well. Their instant results are called "miracles."

So on the other side I am truly in "heaven," where I can manifest anything I desire.

Yes. And what you desire is to come to Full Knowing of who you are, and then to re-create yourself anew in the next grandest version of that. This is the desire of all life. It is called growth. It is termed evolution.

You will want to know all there is to know about being alive, being you, being Divine. So this time in "heaven," or the spiritual realm, is pure joy. Life in the physical realm can be pure joy as well, it is just that most souls do not know this. They have forgotten who they really are.

It is difficult to describe the activity of your soul in the spiritual realm in much greater detail because of the limitation of your present level of consciousness. I can tell you that it is a time of great Knowing. Yet there will come a moment when Knowing will not be enough. The soul will seek to experience what it Knows of Itself in its new idea about Itself. This, it understands, can occur only in the physical world.

So the soul returns to physicality.

Yes. Happily and joyfully. Your soul returns to the Core of Your Being, and once again, on the return journey, it responds to the Holy Inquiry: Do you Know what you wish to Know? Do you choose now to return to physicality?

When the answer/thought/feeling is yes, your soul makes another choice: To return to physicality in the same lifeline, or as a different physical being.

Is the soul limited to Earth as a destination? Or can the soul return to physicality in some other form, on some other planet or in some other location in the universe?

As we discussed earlier in this conversation, there are many routes through the Space/Time Continuum—

In *Stranger in a Strange Land* Robert Heinlein said there are so many "when/wheres"—

Yes. He put it perfectly. And you may choose any one that you wish. Having done so, you enter once more into Total Immersion, which attenuates your life energy so that you may enter into the experience that you call "birth."

Thank you.

Thank you for this description and thank you for this entire conversation. I know that it has contained a lot of "process descriptions"—explanations through metaphor, science, and metaphysics of the cosmology of all of life and of "how everything works"—but it has also given me some wonderful spiritual insights and deeper understandings and awarenesses that have brought me comfort, and that I hope bring comfort to many others—especially people who are dealing with the death of a loved one, or those who, themselves, are approaching death.

It is the opportunity of every true minister of God (and you are all just that—ordained or otherwise) to bring comfort to the dying.

Yes. And having said that, it is sometimes difficult to find words to say to those who are grieving the loss of a loved one. A woman named Sheila wrote this to me a few years ago . . .

Dear Neale:

My brother Chuck died several years ago, when he was only twenty-seven, and I can't seem to stop grieving. Every day I think of him, everything I see reminds me of him. Nothing seems to matter to me anymore. I am chronically depressed. Can you help?

Sheila, WI

What can the average person say to someone like this? That is the question. After all, we are not all trained ministers. We are not all licensed counselors. We have not all spent years in the helping professions.

Well, what did *you* say?

I answered the best way I could, based on what my conversation with God has given me. I said . . .

Dear Sheila,

I am sorry for your loss and I understand your grief. There are some things that I would like to tell you, though, that may help you to repaint this memory on the canvas of your mind, so that when you look at it, you are not always sad.

First, you must know that Chuck has not died; that death is a fiction and a lie and never, ever takes place. That is number one, and that is something you must take into your Self as a truth of the highest order for any of the rest of this to make sense.

Second, if we accept that Chuck is not the thing you call "dead," but is, in fact, very much alive, then we must ask ourselves: Where is he? What is he doing? And, of course, is he happy?

We'll answer the last question first. Chuck was never happier, nor more joyful, than he was at the moment of his transition from this earthly life. For in that moment he knew once again the grandest freedom, the greatest joy, the most wondrous truth—the truth of his own being, and of its oneness with All That Is.

Separation ended for Chuck in that moment, and his reunification with the All of Everything was a glorious moment in the heavens and the earth. It was a time, indeed, for celebration, not for mourning, yet mourning is understandable, given our limited awareness of what is truly happening, as well as the magnitude of our own personal loss, which we are naturally experiencing.

After a period of very natural grief, which we must be good enough to give ourselves, it then becomes our choice to stay in that place of utter devastation and mourning, or to move to a larger awareness and a grander truth, which allows us to smile—yes, even at the thought of his departure, however early, however abruptly, although nothing is "early" or "abrupt" in God's timetable, but all is perfectly timed.

Should we choose to move to this larger awareness, we are then free to celebrate in fullness the life which was Chuck's, the gift he bestowed upon all those he touched, and the wonder of his beingness and his love even now.

We do this most by allowing Chuck himself to be completely free. Which brings us to the first question in the trio above: where is Chuck now? In *CwG, Book 3* it was revealed to me that in the world of the absolute in which God dwells, we are all everywhere. That is, there is no "here" or "there," there is simply "everywhere." Thus, in human terms, it is possible to say that we can be in more than one place at a time. We can be two places, or three places, or any place we wish to be, having any experience we choose to have. For this is the nature of God, and of all God's beings.

And what experience do we choose to have, among others? The experience of oneness and empathy for those we love, just as we did while in bodily form. What that means is that Chuck loves you even now, not in some theoretical sense, but in a very real sense, with a living love that can and will never die. And that eternal and everlasting love causes Chuck (part of the essence that is Chuck) to come to you, to be with you, with the very thought of him. For the thought of one who loves us is an attraction and a pull that the essence of a being cannot and will not deny, and will never ignore.

Chuck is with you even now, as you are reading this, for you have him in mind, and a part of him is very much there with you. If you are very quiet, and very sensitive to the moment, you will even be able to sense him, feel him . . . maybe even "hear" him.

This is true of all people everywhere, and it explains the thousands and thousands of reports received every year of "visits" by departed loved ones to those who remain behind, reports that psychiatrists, ministers, doctors, and healers of every kind have become very used to hearing, and no longer question.

Often what happens is that the essence of the beingness that flew to us at the very thought of it arrives in our space full of love and compassion, and complete openness with us. That openness will allow the essence of our loved one to know and understand completely what we are feeling and experiencing.

If we think of that person with sadness, grief, and pain, the sadness we experience will be known to that essence. And since that essence is now pure love, it will lovingly seek to heal our sadness, for it will find it impossible not to want to do so.

If, on the other hand, we think of that person with joy and celebration, our joy will be known to the essence of the person we have so deeply loved, and that essence will then feel free to move into its next grand adventure, knowing that all is okay with us. It will come back, to be sure. It will return each time it is thought of.

Yet its visits will be joyous dances in our mind; wondrous, sparkling connections; brief, yet shining moments; smiles made whole. Then the essence will whisk away once more, gladdened by the thought of your love and your celebration of its life, feeling complete in its interaction with you, although by no means ended.

Now in the process of helping us to heal our grief and sadness, the essence of our loved one will stop at nothing, using any tool, borrowing any device, employing any method at its disposal (including, perhaps, a letter like this from a total stranger) to bring us the message of its unremitting joy in the place of its current residing, and the truth of the perfection of the process of life and transition.

When we can celebrate the perfection, we allow the essence and the soul of our loved one to celebrate it as well, releasing it to the unspeakable wonders of its larger reality, honoring its presence in our lives, in its former physical form, now in this moment, and even forevermore.

Celebrate, celebrate, celebrate! No more sadness, no more mourning, for no tragedy has truly befallen anyone. Yet special remembrance with smiles and tears, yes, but tears of joy at the wonder of Who We Are, of who Chuck is, and of the unspeakable love of a God who could have created all this for us.

Celebrate, Sheila. Give yourself and Chuck, and all those whose lives are touched by both of you, the gift of a lifetime: the gift of joy replacing sorrow, of gladness overtaking the pain of loss, of genuine gratefulness, and of peace at last.

God's blessings, not the least of which are Chuck's life and Chuck's presence with you even now, surround you, Sheila. Go now, and be Who You Really Are. And smile.

Chuck would have it no other way.

Blessings,
Neale

That was a wonderful reply. I am sure that Sheila found it very, very comforting.

Yes, but was it true? Or am I just making it all up?

Yes.

Yes, what?

Yes to both questions. It is true *because* you are making it all up. You may have it any way that you wish.

You keep telling me that, and I keep wanting to have it be a certain way because *that's the way it really is.*

But that *is* the way it really is.
That is the way it "really is" because you keep creating it that way. If you wish to create it another way, it will be another way.
This can be said, incidentally, about the whole of your life, on earth as it is in heaven.

Well, if I am really creating my life and the life around me the way that I choose, then I choose for all of us to truly embrace the call to our own ministry in the world. I am so inspired by people such as Joan Beck (whose name I've changed to protect this person's identity), who gifted me in January 2003 with a personal sharing of how the death of her son changed her life.

Jason—her firstborn son—was eighteen, a senior in high school. He tragically drowned the first day of swim class. His death devastated Joan, her family, and her community.

Joan explained that she never realized just how physical the healing of her grief could be. Two short days after Jason's death, she felt him with her. She says that she couldn't have made it through the heartbreaking experience without him there.

Joan's experience of connecting with her son spiritually instigated her journey to understand the meaning behind Jason's death. As the daughter of a United Methodist minister, she believed that God was present, but expecting her to take care of her own life. But she just couldn't figure out why her beloved son had to die. After all, Joan had always been a good mother, teaching her children right from wrong.

After Jason physically passed away, Joan explained to me that her son remained a partner in her search for answers. He would guide her, even when she resisted the truth. Her ability to forgive the gym teacher is one example of the way Jason continued to play a role in Joan's life.

Joan had never had much contact with the gym teacher, but after Jason's death, she kept running into him. Jason helped Joan realize that forgiving the gym teacher was the proper course of action. Now she feels liberated from her feelings of anger. Although she worries that some people might think she's nuts, she takes solace in the fact that she's found a new way of life.

When Joan shared her story with me, I was touched by her experience, and I thanked her for sharing it with me. Then I said . . .

> I know, Joan, how desperately you must have felt when Jason died, and I am so glad that he found a way to stay connected with you, so that you might have his help in dealing with all of this—and in leading you to larger and larger truths.
>
> I am clear now that this was Jason's purpose from the very beginning. Each of us comes into each other's lives for a reason and a purpose. It almost always has to do with some level of spiritual growth. You have also come into the life of this gym teacher for the same reason. As terrible as you must

feel about what happened, I can imagine what he must feel as well. Even though he may not show it, I am certain that he is devastated inside. This happened on his watch. He can never live that down, never do anything to change it. He will cry to himself at night for many, many years, I am sure.

I hope that you have not only forgiven him in your heart, but talked with him in person, and shared your human love with him, to let him know that you understand how terrible he must feel (even if he isn't showing it, I repeat), and that you want him to know not that you "forgive" him (which makes it sound like he did something "wrong" for which he is "guilty," but that you are letting him "off the hook") but that you have no *need* to forgive him, because you are clear that he is a good man, that he did nothing on purpose or with malicious intent, and that what happened was a tragedy that just happened. It just happened. These things occur in life. These things happen. And no one is "at fault" in things such as this.

Tell him that you understand this, and that you hope he has been able to get on with his life as you are now getting on with yours, still ready and able to bring joy and love and laughter and happiness into the lives of others.

Yes, and tell him that Jason wants him to remember always the many hundreds of young men whose lives he has touched in positive and important ways—and that his days of doing that are far from over. And that to learn how to live with a mistake is to transform tragedy into blessing, healing all of humankind, for all of us have made mistakes in life, and all of us are human, and all of us are also capable of giving and bringing much love to the world, and all of us will, if we allow ourselves to.

Tell him things like that, for this man needs to be healed of his wound, and you are one of the most powerful people who can help him do that. Yes?

Love and hugs ...
Neale

This is how Joan can be a real minister. You do not have to be "ordained" to be a minister in the world. God has ordained you by virtue of your being alive. You can be—and are—a minister right now. Every day, if you look for it, you will find a chance to bring your ministry of healing and of love to someone new.

What can I say to those who are dying? Until now this has always been a tough one for me. For most of us, I would imagine. What comfort can I offer them?

If you find people who believe that forgiveness is what is required to make them "worthy of heaven," offer them forgiveness—and tell them that God does so also.

If you find people who believe that they will be step-ping right into the arms of God and their loved ones after their death, offer them confirmation—and tell them that God does so also.

If you find people who believe there is no life of any kind after death, offer them an alternative idea—and tell them that God does so also.

God does so through many events of life, in a thousand different voices during a hundred different moments, heard by all those who will truly listen.

This conversation, offered to you and to all of humanity, is one of those events.

And so I invite you here to offer this prayer to those who are dying:

The God of your understanding is with you now, even in this hour, at this precise moment. If you have no understanding of God, that will not matter. God is still here, in this place, with you right now, whispering to your soul, "You are welcome, whenever you are ready to come Home."

You shall not be turned away, not for any cause or reason. If there be cause or reason you believe to be valid, God—should you want God to—in this moment invalidates it. God—should you want God to—in this moment erases it. God—should you want God to—in this moment makes all paths clear, all roads straight, saying, "Make way for my beloved, who chooses to be Home with God."

This prayer is offered for you, wonderful child of the universe, as you embark on the most joyful journey you have ever taken, filled with wondrous surprises. A journey into the greatest happiness you have ever known, and the grandest experience you will ever have.

Dream now of glorious things. Dream of every fantasy come true. Dream of every pain disappearing, of everything of which time has robbed you being given back to you again. Dream of seeing loved ones once more—those who have gone before and those who will follow.

Know for a certainty that when you leave here, you will

be again with all those who have held a place in your heart and have gone before. And do not worry about those you leave behind, for you will see them, too, again and again, and love them, too, again and again, through all eternity, and even in the present moment. For there can be no separation where there is love, and no waiting where there is only Now.

Smile, then, at the joyful anticipation of what is in store. These gifts have been laid up for you, and God has only been waiting for you to return Home to receive them. Peace, joy, and love are you, and are yours, now and always. So it is, and so it shall be, for ever and ever. Amen.

Your ancestors walk with you. Your heirs stand beside you,
watching your decisions on their behalf.

Thank you, dear God, for that wonderful, wonderful prayer. I hope that people everywhere, all over the world, will use it if they feel it would serve the moment, and bring peace and comfort, hope and understanding, to the dying.

But wait, please. There is still something that I, myself, need to understand.

Did I hear you correctly? What did you mean when you said that we will see our loved ones who follow us in death "even in the present moment"?

Do you remember when, early in this conversation, you talked about Andrew Parker's wife, Pip, and you asked me a question about her?

Yes. I asked you if she wanted to get cancer at that early stage in her life. I asked if she really *chose,* as a matter of free will, to leave that soon, to die so young. I said that something like this would be really hard to accept by her husband, her children, and members of her family. They would ask, with deep sorrow, I am sure, *Why would Pip want to leave us like that?*

And do you remember what I said?

Yes, you said, "I have an answer that may shock you."

I have saved two Remembrances for the end of our conversation. These are the most joyous, the most wondrous Remembrances of all.

The first of these is . . .

THE SEVENTEENTH REMEMBRANCE
In death you will be greeted by all of your loved ones—those who have died before you and those who will die after you.

These souls will comfort you as you release your attachment to the physical world, gently guiding you into the spiritual realm. You need never be alone, ever, nor are you ever alone now.

I am so grateful to know this. "Aloneness" on the journey is my greatest fear.

You are never alone, and you cannot *be* alone, by the very nature of who you are. For you are not an individual, but an Individuation of the All. You are a part of All of Us Who Live, and all of us who live have an investment in the experience of You. Your ancestors walk with you. Your heirs stand beside you, watching your decisions on their behalf. We are all with you always, and you with us. It takes but your belief to Know that we are there.

Yes, but this I don't understand. This last Remembrance I cannot comprehend. Do you mean that when I close my eyes in death and open them again in the Afterlife, everyone I have ever loved—*including those I have just left behind*—will be there?

> If you want them to be, they will be. If you believe
> they will be, if you so much as hope that they will be,
> you will be aware of their presence beside you.

But . . . look, as I already told you, I've heard it said many times that the souls of those who have *preceded* me in death will be waiting for me when I "cross over." You said that yourself, earlier in this conversation. But I've *never* heard it said that the people who are alive with me *now,* who are alive at the moment of my death, will be there to greet me. How can this be?

> Such is the wonder of the Ultimate Reality that,
> though it may be experienced as a long while for
> those who remain living in physicality within the illu-
> sion of time, it will be in your own Moment of Now
> that you will be reunited.

But . . . I thought that I would be there to greet *them* when *they* die. I mean, if I am one of *their* loved ones, wouldn't I be waiting for them when they die?

> Yes, you would . . . and you will.

Gosh, I'm sorry, I'm not doing such a good job of following this. If I am waiting for them as *they* cross over, and they are already there for me when I cross over, how can . . . what is the sequence here?

> Your greeting of each other at the end of your phys-
> ical lives is *sequentaneous.*

But when a thing is sequential *and* simultaneous, which do I
experience? You never explained this to me before. Do I experience that one thing is happening after another, or do I experience
everything happening instantly?

> Whichever you choose. You may look at an individual
> image in your "mural," or you may step back and look
> at the entire mural at once. It is all a matter of perspec-
> tive. And you may choose any perspective that serves
> you. You may take any perspective that pleases you.

The implications of this are enormous. It's almost as if, when
my life is over, *everyone's* life is over. When *I* die, *everyone* dies. That
doesn't seem fair.

> There is nothing unfair about it. Injustice and unfair-
> ness are not possible in Ultimate Reality.
>
> It may be many years before your presently living
> loved ones die, yet those years will be compressed into
> less than an instant in the place of No Time. If you wish
> to step back from the mural and see the whole pic-
> ture, you will experience them joining you in the After-
> life in "no time at all."
>
> That is why I said before that if you *believe* that your
> loved ones—*all* of your loves ones—will be with you in
> the Afterlife just as you cross over, if you so much as
> *hope* that they will be, you will be aware of their pres-
> ence beside you. Belief creates perspective, and hope

distances you from your worst imagining, allowing you to see a larger picture.

Oh, my gosh, this is theologically so new, so . . . *startling.* I have never heard this anywhere. I mean, it's just not something I ever imagined.

> That is a perfect description of the Kingdom of God.
>
> I tell you now, you will be together with all the souls with whom you have ever traveled, those you are traveling with now, and *those souls you will travel with in the future.*

My *future companions* will be there?

> If you want them there, yes.
>
> Nothing will happen that you do not choose. Remember, "heaven" is getting what you want. "Hell" is getting what you don't want. There has been a lot of theology created around both of those words, but in the end, that's it. And "hell" does not even exist unless you create it yourself—which means that you are *still* getting what you want! And if you do create your own hell, it disappears the moment you don't want it anymore.

So, in truth, *heaven is all there is.*

> Indeed, this could be the whole of your theology: Heaven is all there is.

Use the events of today to create the promise of tomorrow.

I am so enthralled with this idea! But—and maybe I am "thinking" about this way too much, BUT—if I am to also be joined in this heaven by those souls with whom I will go through future lives, that would mean that I am going through *all* of my lives—including *this one*—with souls that I have known . . . *ahead of time.*

> Yes, that is what it would mean. Have you never met a person and just knew that you've known them before?

Yes, many ti— Ohmygodwhatareyoutellingme?

> This is just the beginning of the wonder and the glory, my beautiful child, just the beginning. For Shakespeare had it right when he said, "There are more things in heaven and earth, Horatio, than are dreamt of in your philosophy."

Have I not told you that in my Kingdom there are many mansions? Have I not said, ye are Gods?

I tell you, you will *all* gather together, you Souls of Antiquity. You will all meet and love again. You will all join once more, and always, in the Sacred Circle of Co-Creation.

And the soul partners of all your lifetimes will surround you and shower you with love as you respond to the Holy Inquiry: *Do you wish now to go on? Are you complete with this present experience of Divinity?*

What an incredible revelation!

Oh, my wonder, my child, my breathtaking creation, I have told you almost nothing yet. I have things to show you that will make even this commonplace. And the first thing I will have to show you when you leave this life is your glorious self. *As you were originally created* will you be seen, in the mirror of your own love. For you will love yourself again, even as you did when you were allowed to, in heaven. And you will be whole again, and young again, and you will move into the spiritual realm with all the zest and spirit of your most exciting time. You will experience yourself as in the days of your earthly youth, and it will be as if no time has passed at all—which is *exactly what has happened.*

I must ask you a final question—something we have not touched upon at all throughout this entire dialogue. What about the death of children? Do they experience the same things we have been talking about here?

They do, and in a very gentle way. Death is very kind to children, because children rarely move into death holding all sorts of preconceived negative notions about what happens afterward. They are pure. They have only just come from the spiritual realm. They are not that far removed from the Core of Their Being. They have just emerged from the Essence. And so small children move through the first stages of death very quickly and return almost immediately into Mergence with the Essence.

But when they emerge from that, and they experience the moment of the Holy Inquiry, do they continue on their journey as tiny little children, or whatever age child they were when they left their body?

They are given a moment of the Biggest Free Choice they will ever make—the same choice that all souls face before entering the spiritual realm. They may go on with their lives retaining the identity with which they left their last experience of physical life, or they may create a new identity. All souls have this choice.

It should be said that children "grow up" in the Afterlife. That is, they become fully aware and fully conscious of all that is going on, and of Ultimate Reality. They know why they came to the earth and they know why they left as early as they did. If they feel complete with all of that, they will move on, in whatever form they choose. If they do not feel complete, they will have the same opportunity to "come back to life" as any other soul. The

process is the same for all souls, no matter what the age
of their body when they leave the physical world.

But now I should like to say something about the
agenda of children who die at a very young age.

Yes, please. I would very much like to know about this.

Those souls who enter the body and leave the body
within a very short period—children who die in child-
birth, for instance, or at a very tender age—inevitably
do so in service to the agenda of another, at a very
high level.

All souls come to physicality to serve their individual
agenda, but that agenda may very well have little to do,
specifically, with themselves, and everything to do with
the agenda of others. The soul who returns as an avatar
or master, for instance, does so for the joy of experiencing Itself as that—and knows that the best way to do
this is to serve the agenda of others almost exclusively.

The agenda of others in this case may be to remember Who They Really Are and, at some level, to experience that. The avatar or master serves that agenda in
the living of his or her life.

Similarly, many souls come to earth to experience
the joy of serving the agenda of others in another way.
In some cases, they are required to leave early in order
to do that. This is never, however, a tragedy for that
soul. They have *agreed* to leave early.

You mean we have agreements with other souls? We have
"contracts"?

Yes. Remember that I told you, all the souls you have ever loved will be waiting for you at the time of your death. These include the souls who have preceded you in death, as well as those who have followed you. You will open your "eyes" when you "cross over" to find *everyone there*—just as they will find *you there* when they cross over. You will all be there for each other in the Only Moment There Is.

We'll meet in the same when/where.

Exactly. And you will joyously celebrate all that you have co-created in order that you might, each of you, know your Self as Who You Really Are, and experience that. You will then enter into a "contract" or an agreement with each other on what you will each do in your next *sequentaneous* expression. As always, you will choose to experience this next expression as if it were happening sequentially—and, as always, it will be occurring simultaneously.

Now you asked a while ago about angels, and whether angels ever return to earth in physicality, and I wonder if you remember my answer.

Of course. You said that they do, all the time.

We are talking here about children who die very young.

They are *angels?*

Every soul who comes to the body to serve the agenda of others is an angel—and every child who has died very young has done so to bring a gift to another. That gift may not be understood for some time by parents and others who are, naturally, deeply grieving. But I promise you that as time goes by and healing occurs, the gift will be seen, it will be received, and the work of that little sweetheart—who could *only* be described as an angel—will have been accomplished.

That is a very healing thing to say. That is a very gentle and healing notion.

It is not merely a notion. It is the state of things. It is how things are. It is what is so.

I am so grateful to know this, and to know everything that you have told me in my Conversations with God. This ongoing dialogue with you has changed my life, and touched the lives of millions around the world as well. I don't know what to say. I know this is our final conversation . . .

Our final conversation *in public*. I will always be with you. Always. As your loved ones are always with you. They hover about you now, some in physical form, some as spirit guides and angels. Yet they are *all* angels. Even those you have imagined to be opposing you, even those you have imagined to be your enemies. All have appeared in your world with a Divine reason and for a Divine purpose: that you might know and choose, express and experience, become and fulfill, Who You Really Are.

Know this, therefore: Life on this planet is your greatest treasure, created for you as a context within

which you might make the next most glorious decision about your Self. And know also that to assist you
in this choice *I have sent you nothing but angels.*

You have told me this before. I could not hear you. My life was
such a mess, I had to find someone to blame. The world was so
near to destruction, I had to find *someone* to make wrong.

Yet have I not said, judge not, and neither condemn?
Therefore, be a Light unto the darkness, and curse it
not. For all that has come to pass has come to bring
passage for you, into the world and the experience of
your most wondrous imagining.

Use the events of today to create the promise of
tomorrow, and use your experience of Now to produce the wonder of Forever.

With this, let our public conversation end. You said
early in our dialogue that you have not yet accomplished what you set out to accomplish. Now you have.
Almost. You only have to remember now how to love.
Completely, not just a little bit. Selflessly, not only when
it's in your own best interest.

That is enough for you to focus on now, so you can
allow this public conversation to end. For you have
brought to its conclusion, with this final information
about the cosmology of all of life and of life after
death, a dialogue that is meant for all of humanity, and
that is enough. You have given this process ten years
of your life, and that is enough. You have changed
the world's mind about God, and about Life, and that
is enough.

Yes, but not all of the world, not the whole world.

The whole world *has* changed. I promise you.

The New Revelations and Tomorrow's God have been embraced by people everywhere, and because of your work and the work of many others like you—the teachers, the authors, the speakers and singers of songs, the healers and ministers, the tellers of stories in murals that move, the mommies and the daddies who cuddled their young in the embrace of real and abiding love, the workers in the vineyard and all the messengers who have been deeply committed to changing the way life is lived upon the earth—the World Entire has begun its remarkable transformation.

In time, that transformation will be complete. In Time/No Time, it has already been accomplished.

For this has been your will, and mine. And in this world of our creation, Our will is done.

Are you surprised?

A surprising moment will be the moment that you first enter the spiritual realm and discover that you may create, with the speed of your thought, anything at all. And that you may come to Know what you have created sequentially *or* simultaneously, as you choose. Oh, yes, what a surprise this will be!

And yet, the biggest surprise and the biggest wonder will still be to come. Only after you choose to re-create yourself anew, only after you decide, with the souls of all your loved ones around you, how you next wish to experience the wonder and the glory of who you are, only in the moment of that choice will the totality of your awareness be opened to ...

THE EIGHTEENTH REMEMBRANCE

Free Choice is the act of pure creation, the signature of God, and your gift, your glory, and your power forever and ever.

You may exercise this power both in the spiritual realm and in the physical world. With your thoughts, with your words, and with your deeds will you do so. You are doing so now, even in this present moment. Therefore in this glorious time of Now/Always, re-create your Self anew in the next grandest version of the greatest vision you ever held about Who You Are.

And know this, finally: Whatever you choose and wherever you are, you always have the ability to instantly be ...

Home with God.

So be it.

AFTERWORD

My dear and wonderful friends . . .

Thank you for taking this journey with me. I am so very grateful.

I am grateful because I know that it has taken courage and an enormous willingness to be open to new thoughts and new ideas about God and about Life for you to stay with this dialogue for so long. Grateful, also, because I know that now you, too, understand. You, too, remember. You, too, know Who You Really Are. And this can make all the difference in our world.

When I first began this dialogue ten years ago, I felt very much alone. Yet I knew that the messages contained in these extraordinary books were not meant for only me. They were meant for the world entire, and they were meant to *change* the world entire. Our world could benefit from some changing right now if we wish to continue our adventure on this beautiful Earth and enjoy a better life than we have known.

We have gone about as far as we can go in the direction we are now taking. We are beginning to disassemble everything we put together during the long process of our evolution. We can see this gradual deconstruction going on all around us. Yet the die has not been cast, and our future is by no means determined. Indeed, our species stands at the threshold of tomorrow with two distinct possibilities presenting themselves as options. Will we now take a quantum leap forward toward a glorious expression of the collective life with which we have been gifted, truly becoming highly evolved beings? Or will we take a giant step backward toward our own meager beginnings, embracing once again a caveman mentality, and living according to the most primitive priorities?

These are the questions facing humanity today, and I have seen these questions looming before us from the earliest days of my youth. I have felt from those earliest moments that the solution to our most pressing problems was lying right before us, and would be found in the simple rearranging of our most basic assumptions about the life we were living. Today, at the end of a decade of conversations with God, I am certain of that.

Yet this I know also: changing humanity's assumptions about life is not something that can be done easily, or alone. It will take the combined effort of every human being who feels a calling to help create tomorrow. You know right now if you are one of those people.

If you are, you will commit to making the end of this Decade of Dialogue the beginning of a Century of Change. I figure it will take just about 100 years—the rest of my lifetime and yours, and some years beyond—to secure humanity's future. In cosmic terms that's a blink of an eye, but in human terms that's a long-range job, so it's good that we're getting started. Actually, we've begun not a moment too soon, as you can see from even the most casual glance at the world around us.

Our mission, should we choose to accept it, is to change the world's mind about itself. To do that, we have to change our Cultural Story. We have to alter what we keep telling ourselves about who we are, how life is, why we are here on the earth, and what God wants. We have to educate our children in a new way and with new ideas about what it means to be human. And we have to begin all of this by reeducating ourselves.

You know all of this, of course. Deep inside, you already know all of this. That's why you came to this book. You may think you came to it by happenstance or by chance, but of course that is not true, and now you're able to see that. You've opened yourself to this dialogue with Deity, you've allowed yourself to have this conversation with God, so that you could remember what you've always understood at the deepest part of your being—and so that you could gather and form the articulations to help everyone else remember as well.

That is why these *Conversations with God* have happened to me, and that is why they have happened to you.

And so now the real work begins. And you have an important role to play, whether you have four weeks to live, or four months; four years or four decades.

Even those who are very near death—perhaps especially those— have a job they can do. Should they choose to do so, they can share a message by the way in which they die that will deeply impact everyone around them and, therefore, their world. That is one of the main points of this book. *Death,* this final dialogue says, *is an act of creation.*

Likewise, those of us who are continuing to live in our present physical form for a while longer have much that we can contribute to the process by which all souls come to a remembrance of who we are and why we are all here. Having placed ourselves upon the earth to know and experience our true identity, we can accelerate that process by assisting others in knowing and experiencing theirs.

This is the Great Secret of Life. This is the most important corner that we will ever turn as we journey onward to our home with God.

There are many ways that you may undertake this work, and

before I leave you with this final dialogue text I am going to suggest one extraordinary way that you could change your life and
change your world. But first, let's look at some rather simple
things you can do and at some immediately accessible resources
to expand your personal experience of the wonderful energy of
the New Spirituality.

You might choose to generate group energy in exploring the
ideas of the New Spirituality that can free humanity from its old
paradigm of fear and separation, anger and violence, moving into a
more peaceful and joyous expression of life. You could do this by
forming a *Home with God* Study Group. The creation of small groups
that meet informally in people's houses two or three times a month
can go far in helping us all to write a new Cultural Story built on new
beliefs that produce new behaviors in our daily lives. (If you would
like information on a *Home with God* Study Course that can help you
in this process, it may be found at nealedonaldwalsch.com.)

It is by such means that we change the world. Please do not
doubt this. A small handful of people meeting regularly in "cells"
around the globe has already deeply impacted our daily life and
changed our world. The only question remaining is not, can people
meeting quietly in groups change our world, but *how do we want our
world to change?*

One thing I am asked repeatedly wherever I go is: How can I
get the messages from *Conversations with God* across to my children?

I am so happy to tell you that now there is a way, thanks to a
remarkable man named Robert Friedman, who has chosen to pub-
lish a series of children's books based on CwG. The first two books
in this series are *The Little Soul and the Sun* and *The Little Soul and the
Earth.* These books tell the continuing story of The Little Soul and
its adventure in both the spiritual realm and the physical world.

They do so in such a way, and with such beautiful illustrations, that children ages 4 to 7 can easily grasp the deeper meanings they convey.

More adventures of the Little Soul are on the way. All are from Hampton Roads Publishing Company, which Mr. Friedman created just so that he could bring such messages to the world. (I should tell you that it was this man who first took the risk of publishing the initial *Conversations with God* trilogy ten years ago. What now seems commonplace was at that time a gamble. A lot of money and goodwill could have been lost. This did not stop Bob, and the world is the better for his having had that level of courage and commitment.)

For your teenage children or grandchildren you may wish to consider *Conversations with God for Teens.* This book contains right-to-the-point inquiries from teenagers about life as they are living it. I went around the world and onto the internet to inquire of teens, "If you could ask God any question, what would it be?" The extraordinary dialogue in this unique book for young people is the result.

If you would like some beautiful musical reminders of the messages here, may I recommend some places where you may find them? Carly Simon's album of several years ago, *Have You Seen Me Lately?,* contains the extraordinary song "Life Is Eternal," based on the message from Rossiter W. Raymond that I have quoted in this book. Country song stylist Annie Sims has also recorded some very special music, including at least two songs inspired directly by her experience of *Conversations with God.* The achingly beautiful "Go Within," from her album *Half the Moon,* is a deeply moving example. As well, many of the profoundly insightful songs written and performed in recent years by Alanis Morissette speak right from the heart of the Goddess/God within all of us. I am so inspired by the commitment Alanis has made to use her extraordinary gift not only to entertain, but to expand the consciousness of our planet.

I also would like to raise your awareness about a way you can share what the participants in our CwG Spiritual Renewal Retreats have experienced through the years during the very special guided meditations offered by Nancy Fleming Walsch. Many of our participants have told us that these remarkable meditations offered them a method of moving from Knowing to Experiencing who they are, providing a wonderful way to notice their connection to Source. This movement from Knowing to Experiencing is the journey that we have talked about extensively in this book. Three of Nancy's deeply impactful meditations are now on CD in a program called *Your Secret Place*. I highly recommend it to anyone who would like a tool with which to richly explore what it is like to be Home with God.

Information on the *Home with God* Study Course, the *Little Soul* books for children, the music of Annie Sims and Alanis Morissette, the extraordinary guided imageries on the *Your Secret Place* CD, and the Conversations with God Spiritual Renewal Retreats presented around the world may be obtained by going to www.nealedonaldwalsch.com and clicking on the Special Opportunities and Resources page. Yet that is only the beginning.

What I intend that you will take from all of this is that you, *yourself,* can be a powerful force in the creation of our collective tomorrows. The question is not whether you *can,* but whether you *will.*

Yet in order to do so, you must have a tool, a method, a way in which the powerful force that is within you can play its effect on the powerful force that is outside of you. You do have that tool, but you may not be aware of it. It is the tool of individualized realization through collective action. That is, it is the method by which each of us can have our way by gathering with others in a united undertaking directing its efforts toward the same end. I have used this quote before, and I will use it again: "The problem with the world today is that the civil are not organized . . . and the organized are not civil." I believe it was newspaper columnist Jimmy Breslin who penned those words, and he couldn't have been more pithily accurate. Our job, then, is to *get organized.*

Standing in front of an audience of some 750 people in the Netherlands in October 2005, I made a statement quite spontaneously that has since ignited a worldwide undertaking by a select group of extraordinary people. I said to the audience that night, "Look at what a handful of people has done to produce terror in our world. Imagine what a similarly small handful of people could do if they were equally committed to producing peace, love, and joy in our world."

I added, "You give me 1,000 people—ten from the Netherlands, ten from Denmark, ten from France, ten from Germany, ten from Italy . . . 100 from all of Europe, 100 likewise from Korea, China, Japan, and the Far East, 100 from the Middle East, 100 from Africa, 100 from South America, 100 from North America, and so forth . . . just give me 1,000 people spread out like that all over the planet, and we'll change the world."

Then I surprised myself by saying, "In fact, if you want to be one of those people, send me an e-mail at info@The GroupOf1000.com." At that point no such address existed! I had to rush back to my hotel room following the lecture and create it. The next morning when I opened this new e-mailbox, there were 77 messages!

We were on our way.

Now we are moving forward, putting together a worldwide network that will support a remarkable global initiative to help humanity change its mind about itself. We intend to do this by changing our Cultural Story, and we intend to do *that* by changing what we teach ourselves *about* ourselves.

Not everyone who inquires about The Group of 1000 decides to become a member. The requested level of commitment to our world and its future is very, very high. Those who have joined have chosen to make a difference on our planet in a profound and remarkable way.

If you would like to know more about this ground-level spiritual initiative, please write to: info@TheGroupOf1000.com.

I would like to conclude here with a word about traditional religion and its most up-to-date "take" on some of this. I am aware that many members of those traditional religions will be paying attention to this dialogue and to what we are doing here.

Often I wish that some of our traditional religions could see things even a tiny bit differently. So much could change, and millions of people would not have to approach life or death or God with fear, if only traditional religion could stop teaching that God sends us to hell, that it is God who either grants us our reward or condemns us to everlasting damnation on Judgment Day.

Often I think, if only religion could teach that *we are doing this to ourselves.* Then we could eliminate guilt from our consciousness as we approach the moment of death, and we would never create our own "hell" when we move through death's door.

Yet as I think this I just acknowledge that traditional religion *is* changing a great deal with regard to its messages, and I am truly grateful. I see this as a sure and certain sign of our evolution, and I want to acknowledge and honor the breathtaking shift that I have been witnessing in what some modern-day religious leaders have been saying.

I have mentioned in several previous books the remarkable statements made by Pope John Paul II. Hell does not exist as a place, the Pope said. Both "heaven" and "hell" are (in the words of the Pope, not *Conversations with God*!) "states of being."

In talks before an audience of over 8,000 on consecutive Wednesdays in July of 1999, Pope John Paul II took a close look at these ideas of heaven and hell. According to *L'Osservatore Romano*, the newspaper of the Holy See, the Holy Father said, "When the form of this world has passed away, those who have welcomed God into their lives and have sincerely opened themselves to his love, at least at the moment of death, will enjoy that fullness of communion with God which is the goal of human life."

That, of course, is virtually a repeat of what the book you are holding in your hands has said.

"Heaven is the ultimate end and fulfillment of the deepest human longings, the state of supreme, definitive happiness," the Pope went on.

Speaking about hell in his catechesis, the Pope said that care should be taken not to misinterpret the images of hell in Sacred Scripture, and explained that "rather than a place, hell indicates the state of those who freely and definitively separate themselves from God, the source of all life and joy."

I believe that the Pope was inspired directly by Deity in the making of these statements. He surely was aware that his every word was being followed by the whole world. In my own conversations with God it has repeatedly been made clear that hell is not a punishment from God, but is self-created, out of the thoughts of

isolation of human beings who have been taught that they are separate from God.

Furthermore, I have been inspired in this present conversation
to reveal that the ideas and concepts about hell and damnation that
we carry with us through life reproduce themselves in our experience after we die. That is what happens, God has said here, in
the second stage of death, when we experience what we expect to
experience—including hell, if that is our expectation.

In his own remarks in 1999, Pope John Paul II said that hell "is
not a punishment imposed externally by God, but a development of
premises already set by people in this life."

Can you believe that? That is a statement directly from the highest
religious authority in the lives of billions of the world's people, the
temporal and spiritual leader of one of the world's largest religions.

"Hell is a condition resulting from attitudes and actions which
people adopt in this life," John Paul added.

That is, again, precisely what we have been saying here.

The Pope's idea that hell is not a punishment from God, but is
something we are creating ourselves through our thoughts of separation from the Divine, is strikingly similar to a statement made by
evangelist Billy Graham several years ago:

"The only thing I could say for sure is that hell means separation
from God. We are separated from his light, from his fellowship.
That is going to be hell. When it comes to a literal fire, I don't
preach it because I'm not sure about it" *(Time* magazine, 11/15/93).

So what of the reality of a literal "lake of fire" that burns
throughout eternity? The Bible says that the reality of hell is a vital
doctrine (Heb. 6:1, 2). Jude taught that hell is a real, literal place of
fire and torment (Jude 3, 7). The apostle John saw that hell was a
real place (Rev. 14:10; 20:10-15; 21:8). But both Rev. Graham and

Pope John Paul II completely reject this clear teaching of Scripture.

It is wonderful that high-profile religious leaders are beginning to call into question those out-of-date teachings that do not bring us closer to God but push us farther away. And so I happily acknowledge that mainstream religion is awakening. There *is* hope for a brighter tomorrow. We *can* reach critical mass in the sharing with our world of new ideas about God and about Life if we will all join together, using the power of the Internet and of other forms of mass communication, including radio, television, and films.

I intend to use all of those forms in the months and years ahead now that my "assignment" has been altered. As I have said, this is my last dialogue book. It is not, however, the end of my work. God has just changed my "job description," from bringing the message *through* to getting the message *out.* As I embark on this new mission I intend to dream the impossible dream: that humanity will one day hear God's most important statement to all the world . . .

You've got me all wrong.

So far, there has been one unbeatable foe in humanity's long quest for self-realization. That foe has been our own thought about ourselves. It is as Walt Kelly's wonderful comic strip character, Pogo, put it so succinctly: "We have met the enemy, and they is us."

And so I go forward now, even as Don Quixote, seeing myself, all of us, and the world itself through different eyes. . . .

That is an assignment I hope that you will take on as well. God has promised us that humanity's ideas are shifting, and that our dreams can be the dreams that truly change the world. I would like to witness this reality in the Present Moment of my Now. I urge us all, as we continue creating our collective reality within time and space, to join our energies together to produce the new and wondrous outcomes for which we have so long yearned. My spiritual partnership with you in these past ten years of sharing conversations with God is something that I shall never forget. I cherish you and love you in all the when/wheres of my being.

Let us ALL now go forth . . .

> *To dream the impossible dream,*
> *To fight the unbeatable foe,*
> *To bear with unbearable sorrow,*
> *To run where the brave dare not go.*
>
> *To right the unrightable wrong,*
> *To love, pure and chaste from afar,*
> *To try when your arms are too weary,*
> *To reach the unreachable star,*
>
> *This is my quest, to follow that star,*
> *No matter how hopeless, no matter how far,*
> *To fight for the right without question or pause,*
> *To be willing to march into hell for a heavenly cause.*
>
> *And I know if I'll only be true to this glorious quest,*
> *That my heart will lie peaceful and calm, when I'm laid to*
> *   my rest,*
>
> *And the world will be better for this,*
> *That one man, scorned and covered with scars,*
> *Still strove, with his last ounce of courage,*
> *To reach the unreachable star.*

Always and all ways,

Neale Donald Walsch
Ashland, Oregon
Christmas, 2005

REMEMBRANCES

The First Remembrance: Dying is something you do for you.

The Second Remembrance: You are the cause of your own death. This is always true, no matter where, or how, you die.

The Third Remembrance: You cannot die against your will.

The Fourth Remembrance: No path back Home is better than any other path.

The Fifth Remembrance: Death is never a tragedy. It is always a gift.

The Sixth Remembrance: You and God are one. There is no separation between you.

The Seventh Remembrance: Death does not exist.

The Eighth Remembrance: You cannot change Ultimate Reality, but you *can* change your experience of it.

The Ninth Remembrance: It is the desire of All That Is to Know Itself in Its Own Experience. This is the reason for all of Life.

The Tenth Remembrance: Life is eternal.

The Eleventh Remembrance: The timing and the circumstances of death are always perfect.

The Twelfth Remembrance: The death of every person always serves the agenda of every other person who is aware of it. *That is why they are aware of it.* Therefore, no death (and no life) is ever "wasted." No one ever dies "in vain."

The Thirteenth Remembrance: Birth and death are the same thing.

The Fourteenth Remembrance: You are continually in the act of creation, in life and in death.

The Fifteenth Remembrance: There is no such thing as the end of evolution.

The Sixteenth Remembrance: Death is reversible.

The Seventeenth Remembrance: In death you will be greeted by all of your loved ones—those who have died before you and those who will die after you.

The Eighteenth Remembrance: Free Choice is the act of pure creation, the signature of God, and your gift, your glory, and your power forever and ever.